I0439963

Congressional Research Service

Changes in the Arctic: Background and Issues for Congress

Ronald O'Rourke, Coordinator
Specialist in Naval Affairs

August 1, 2012

Congressional Research Service

7-5700

www.crs.gov

R41153

CRS Report for Congress

Prepared for Members and Committees of Congress

Summary

The diminishment of Arctic sea ice has led to increased human activities in the Arctic, and has heightened interest in, and concerns about, the region's future. The United States, by virtue of Alaska, is an Arctic country and has substantial interests in the region. On January 12, 2009, the George W. Bush Administration released a presidential directive, called National Security Presidential Directive 66/Homeland Security Presidential Directive 25 (NSPD 66/HSPD 25), establishing a new U.S. policy for the Arctic region.

Record low extent of Arctic sea ice in 2007 focused scientific and policy attention on its linkage to global climate change, and to the implications of projected ice-free seasons in the Arctic within decades. The Arctic has been projected by several scientists to be perennially ice-free in the late summer by the late 2030s.

The five Arctic coastal states—the United States, Canada, Russia, Norway, and Denmark (of which Greenland is a territory)—are in the process of preparing Arctic territorial claims for submission to the Commission on the Limits of the Continental Shelf. The Russian claim to the enormous underwater Lomonosov Ridge, if accepted, would reportedly grant Russia nearly one-half of the Arctic area. There are also four other unresolved Arctic territorial disputes.

The diminishment of Arctic ice could lead in coming years to increased commercial shipping on two trans-Arctic sea routes—the Northern Sea Route and the Northwest Passage. Current international guidelines for ships operating in Arctic waters are being updated.

Changes to the Arctic brought about by warming temperatures will likely allow more exploration for oil, gas, and minerals. Warming that causes permafrost to melt could pose challenges to onshore exploration activities. Increased oil and gas exploration and tourism (cruise ships) in the Arctic increase the risk of pollution in the region. Cleaning up oil spills in ice-covered waters will be more difficult than in other areas, primarily because effective strategies have yet to be developed.

Large commercial fisheries exist in the Arctic. The United States is currently meeting with other countries regarding the management of Arctic fish stocks. Changes in the Arctic could affect threatened and endangered species. Under the Endangered Species Act, the polar bear was listed as threatened on May 15, 2008. Arctic climate change is also expected to affect the economies, health, and cultures of Arctic indigenous peoples.

Two of the Coast Guard's three polar icebreakers—*Polar Star* and *Polar Sea*—have exceeded their intended 30-year service lives and are currently not operational. The possibility of increased sea traffic through Arctic waters also raises an issue concerning Arctic search and rescue capabilities. On May 12, 2011, representatives from the member states of the Arctic Council signed an agreement on cooperation on aeronautical and maritime search and rescue in the Arctic.

The Arctic has increasingly become a subject of discussion among political leaders of the nations in the region. Although there is significant international cooperation on Arctic issues, the Arctic is also increasingly being viewed by some observers as a potential emerging security issue. In varying degrees, the Arctic coastal states have indicated a willingness to establish and maintain a military presence in the high north. U.S. military forces, particularly the Navy and Coast Guard, have begun to pay more attention to the region.

Contents

Figures

Appendixes

Contacts

Introduction

The diminishment of Arctic sea ice has led to increased human activities in the Arctic, and has heightened interest in, and concerns about, the region's future. Issues such as Arctic sovereignty claims; commercial shipping through the Arctic; Arctic oil, gas, and mineral exploration; endangered Arctic species; and increased military operations in the Arctic could cause the region in coming years to become an arena of international cooperation, competition, or conflict. The United States, by virtue of Alaska, is an Arctic country and has substantial political, economic, energy, environmental, and other interests in the region. Decisions that Congress, the executive branch, foreign governments, international organizations, and commercial firms make on Arctic-related issues could significantly affect these interests.

This report provides an overview of Arctic-related issues for Congress, and refers readers to more in-depth CRS reports on specific Arctic-related issues. Congressional readers with questions about an issue discussed in this report should contact the author or authors of the section discussing that issue. The authors are identified by footnote at the start of each section.

This report does not track legislation on specific Arctic-related issues. For tracking of legislative activity, see the CRS reports relating to specific Arctic-related issues.

Background[1]

Definitions of the Arctic

There are multiple definitions of the Arctic that result in differing descriptions of the land and sea areas encompassed by the term. Policy discussions of the Arctic can employ varying definitions of the region, and readers should bear in mind that the definition used in one discussion may differ from that used in another. This CRS report does not rely on any one definition.

Arctic Circle Definition and Resulting Arctic Countries

The most common and basic definition of the Arctic defines the region as the land and sea area north of the Arctic Circle (a circle of latitude at about 66.34° North). For surface locations within this zone, the sun is generally above the horizon for 24 continuous hours at least once per year (at the summer solstice) and below the horizon for 24 continuous hours at least once per year (at the winter solstice).

The Arctic Circle definition includes the northernmost third or so of Alaska, as well as the Chukchi Sea, which separates that part of Alaska from Russia, and U.S. territorial and Exclusive Economic Zone (EEZ) waters north of Alaska. It does not include the lower two-thirds or so of Alaska or the Bering Sea, which separates that lower part of the state from Russia.

---

[1] Except for the subsection on the Arctic and the U.N. Convention on the Law of the Sea, this section was prepared by Ronald O'Rourke, Specialist in Naval Affairs, Foreign Affairs, Defense, and Trade Division.

Eight countries have territory north of the Arctic Circle: the United States (Alaska), Canada, Russia, Norway, Denmark (by virtue of Greenland, a member country of the Kingdom of Denmark), Finland, Sweden, and Iceland.[2] These eight countries are often referred to as the Arctic countries, and they are the member states of the Arctic Council, an intergovernmental forum established in 1996.[3] A subset of the eight Arctic countries are the five countries that are considered Arctic coastal states: the United States, Canada, Russia, Norway, and Denmark (by virtue of Greenland).

Definition in Arctic Research and Policy Act (ARPA) of 1984

Section 112 of the Arctic Research and Policy Act (ARPA) of 1984 (Title I of P.L. 98-373 of July 31, 1984[4]) defines the Arctic as follows:

> As used in this title, the term "Arctic" means all United States and foreign territory north of the Arctic Circle and all United States territory north and west of the boundary formed by the Porcupine, Yukon, and Kuskokwim Rivers [in Alaska]; all contiguous seas, including the Arctic Ocean and the Beaufort, Bering, and Chukchi Seas; and the Aleutian chain.

This definition, which is codified at 15 U.S.C. 4111,[5] includes certain parts of Alaska below the Arctic Circle, including the Aleutian Islands and portions of central and western mainland Alaska, such as the Seward Peninsula and the Yukon Delta.

Figure 1 below shows the Arctic area of Alaska as defined by ARPA.

---

[2] On November 25, 2008, voters in Greenland approved a referendum for greater autonomy that some observers view as a step toward eventual independence from Denmark. (Alan Cowell, "Greenland Vote Favors Independence," *New York Times*, November 26, 2008.)

[3] For more on the Arctic Council on the Internet, see http://www.arctic-council.org/.

[4] Title II of P.L. 98-373 is the National Critical Materials Act of 1984.

[5] As codified, the definition reads, "As used in this chapter...."

Figure 1. Arctic Area of Alaska as Defined by ARPA

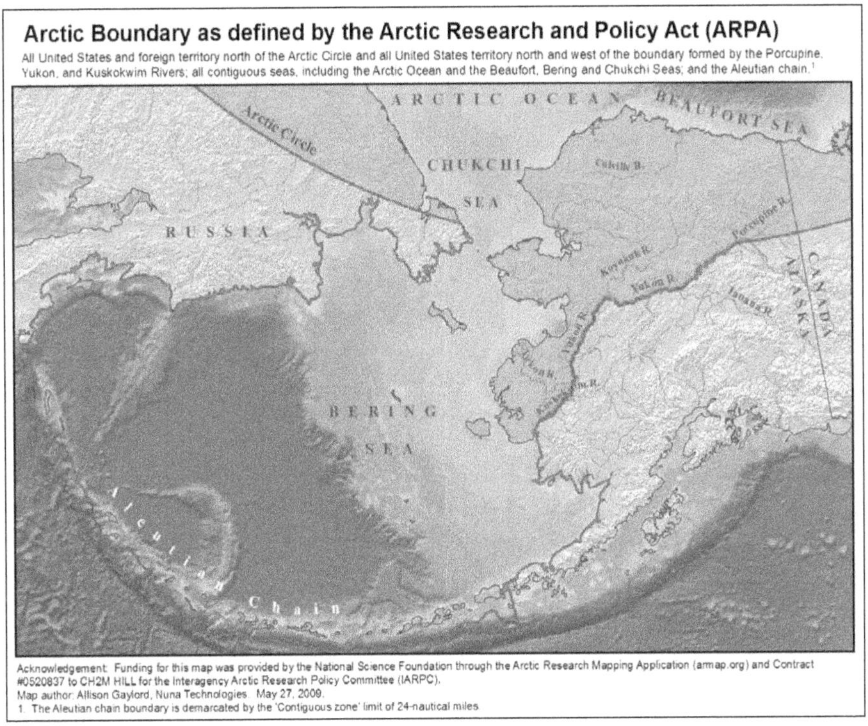
Arctic Boundary as defined by the Arctic Research and Policy Act (ARPA)
All United States and foreign territory north of the Arctic Circle and all United States territory north and west of the boundary formed by the Porcupine, Yukon, and Kuskokwim Rivers; all contiguous seas, including the Arctic Ocean and the Beaufort, Bering and Chukchi Seas; and the Aleutian chain.[1]
ARCTIC OCEAN
BEAUFORT SEA
Arctic Circle
CHUKCHI SEA
RUSSIA
BERING SEA
Aleutian Chain
CANADA
ALASKA
Yukon R.
Porcupine R.
Acknowledgement: Funding for this map was provided by the National Science Foundation through the Arctic Research Mapping Application (armap.org) and Contract #0520837 to CH2M HILL for the Interagency Arctic Research Policy Committee (IARPC).
Map author: Allison Gaylord, Nuna Technologies. May 27, 2009.
1. The Aleutian chain boundary is demarcated by the 'Contiguous zone' limit of 24-nautical miles.

Source: U.S. Arctic Research Commission (http://www.arctic.gov/maps/ARPA_Alaska_only_150dpi.jpg, accessed on December 23, 2011).

Figure 2 shows the entire Arctic area as defined by ARPA.

Figure 2. Entire Arctic Area as Defined by ARPA

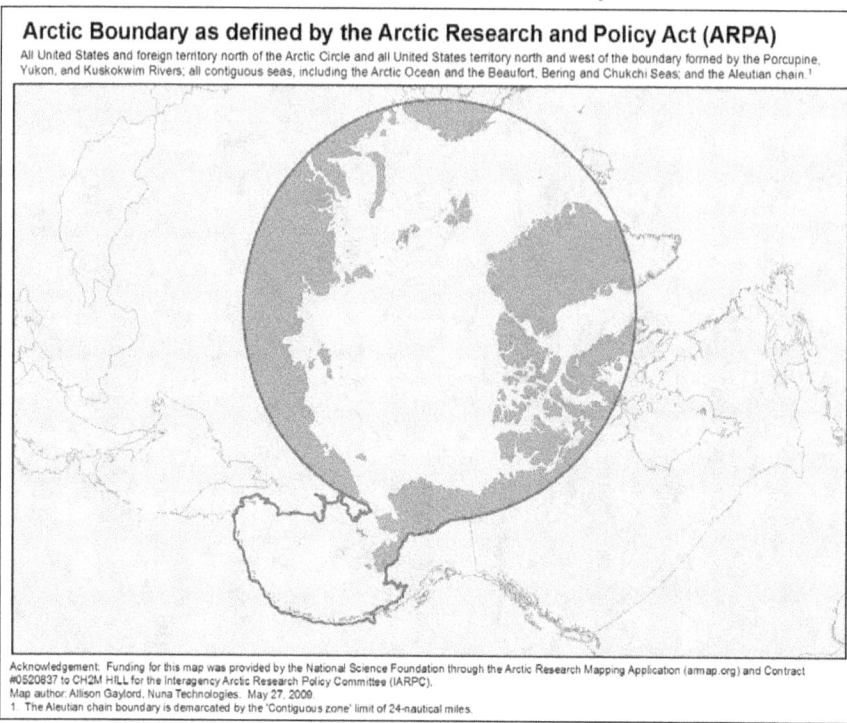

Arctic Boundary as defined by the Arctic Research and Policy Act (ARPA)

All United States and foreign territory north of the Arctic Circle and all United States territory north and west of the boundary formed by the Porcupine, Yukon, and Kuskokwim Rivers; all contiguous seas, including the Arctic Ocean and the Beaufort, Bering and Chukchi Seas; and the Aleutian chain.[1]

Acknowledgement: Funding for this map was provided by the National Science Foundation through the Arctic Research Mapping Application (amap.org) and Contract #0520837 to CH2M HILL for the Interagency Arctic Research Policy Committee (IARPC).
Map author: Allison Gaylord, Nuna Technologies. May 27, 2009.
1. The Aleutian chain boundary is demarcated by the 'Contiguous zone' limit of 24-nautical miles.

Source: U.S. Arctic Research Commission (http://www.arctic.gov/maps/ARPA_Polar_150dpi.jpg, accessed on December 23, 2011).

Other Definitions

Other definitions of the Arctic are based on factors such as average temperature, the northern tree line, the extent of permafrost on land, the extent of sea ice on the ocean, or jurisdictional or administrative boundaries.[6] A definition based on a climate-related factor could circumscribe differing areas over time as a result of climate change.

The 10° C isotherm definition of the Arctic defines the region as the land and sea area in the northern hemisphere where the average temperature for the warmest month (July) is below 10° Celsius, or 50° Fahrenheit. This definition results in an irregularly shaped Arctic region that excludes some land and sea areas north of the Arctic Circle but includes some land and sea areas south of the Arctic Circle. This definition currently excludes all of Finland and Sweden, as well as

---

[6] For discussions and (in some cases) maps, see Susan Joy Hassol, *Impacts of a Warming Arctic* [Executive Summary]. Cambridge, Cambridge University Press, 2004, p. 4. Available online at http://amap.no/acia/; Oran R. Yong and Niels Einarsson, *Arctic Human Development Report*, Stefansson Arctic Institute, Akureyri, Iceland, 2004, pp. 17-18, available online at http://www.svs.is/AHDR/AHDR%20chapters/English%20version/Chapters%20PDF.htm; and Hugo Ahlenius, editor in chief, et al. *Vital Arctic Graphics, People and Global Heritage on Our Last Wild Shores*, UNEP/GRID-Arendal, Arendal, Norway, p. 6, available online at http://www.grida.no/publications/vg/arctic/.

some of Alaska above the Arctic Circle, while including virtually all of the Bering Sea and Alaska's Aleutian Islands.[7]

The definition of the Arctic adopted by the Arctic Monitoring and Assessment Programme (AMAP)—a working group of the Arctic Council—"essentially includes the terrestrial and marine areas north of the Arctic Circle (66°32' N), and north of 62° N in Asia and 60° N in North America, modified to include the marine areas north of the Aleutian chain, Hudson Bay, and parts of the North Atlantic, including the Labrador Sea."[8] The AMAP website includes a map showing the Arctic Circle, 10° C isotherm, tree line, and AMAP definitions of the Arctic.[9]

Some observers use the term "high north" as a way of referring to the Arctic. Some observers make a distinction between the "high Arctic"—meaning, in general, the colder portions of the Arctic that are closer to the North Pole—and other areas of the Arctic that are generally less cold and further away from the North Pole, which are sometimes described as the low Arctic or the subarctic.

U.S. Arctic Research

Arctic Research and Policy Act (ARPA) of 1984, As Amended

The Arctic Research and Policy Act (ARPA) of 1984 (Title I of P.L. 98-373 of July 31, 1984[10]) "provide[s] for a comprehensive national policy dealing with national research needs and objectives in the Arctic."[11] The act, among other things

- made a series of findings concerning the importance of the Arctic and Arctic research;

- established the U.S. Arctic Research Commission (USARC) to promote Arctic research and recommend Arctic research policy;

- designated the National Science Foundation (NSF) as the lead federal agency for implementing Arctic research policy;

- established the Interagency Arctic Research Policy Committee (IARPC) to develop a national Arctic research policy and a five-year plan to implement that policy, and designated the NSF representative on the IARPC as its chairperson;[12] and

---

[7] A map showing the line that results from 10° isotherm definition is available online at https://www.cia.gov/library/publications/the-world-factbook/reference_maps/pdf/arctic.pdf.

[8] Discussion entitled "Geographical Coverage," available online at http://www.amap.no/ (click on "About AMAP" and then the tab "Geographical coverage.")

[9] Discussion entitled "Geographical Coverage," available online at http://www.amap.no/ (click on "About AMAP" and then the tab "Geographical coverage.")

[10] Title II of P.L. 98-373 is the National Critical Materials Act of 1984.

[11] These words are taken from the official title of P.L. 98-373. (Arctic Research and Policy Act of 1984 is the short title of Title I of P.L. 98-373.) The remainder of P.L. 98-373's official title relates to Title II of the act, the short title of which is the National Critical Materials Act of 1984.)

[12] The IARPC currently includes more than a dozen federal agencies, departments, and offices. Additional information on the IARPC is available on the Internet at http://www.nsf.gov/od/opp/arctic/iarpc/start.jsp.

- defined the term "Arctic" for purposes of the act.

The Arctic Research and Policy Act of 1984 was amended by P.L. 101-609 of November 16, 1990. For the texts of the Arctic Research and Policy Act of 1984 and P.L. 101-609, see **Appendix A** and **Appendix B**, respectively.

FY2012 NSF Budget Request For Arctic Research

NSF—the lead federal agency for implementing Arctic research policy (see "Arctic Research and Policy Act (ARPA) of 1984, As Amended")—carries out Arctic research activities through its Division of Arctic Sciences (ARC), which forms part of NSF's Office of Polar Programs (OPP). NSF is requesting a total of $477.41 million for OPP for FY2012, including $112.94 million for ARC.[13] NSF states in its budget request that OPP

> is the primary U.S. supporter of fundamental research in polar regions. In addition, NSF provides interagency leadership for U.S. activities in polar regions. In the Arctic, NSF helps coordinate research planning as directed by the Arctic Research Policy Act of 1984. The NSF Director chairs the Interagency Arctic Research Policy Committee created for this purpose, which is now directly overseen by the President's National Science and Technology Council....
>
> Environmental change in parts of the Arctic and Antarctic is occurring faster than anywhere else in the world, and has a wide variety of regional and global impacts. These impacts include coastal erosion, economically significant changes in terrestrial and marine ecosystems, sea ice changes with effects on planetary albedo, ecosystems and shipping activities, thawing permafrost that compromises civil infrastructure and has the potential to increase releases of methane, a potent greenhouse gas, and contributions to global sea level rise by melting land ice. The human response to these changes also have local to global implications.
>
> The thrust of research supported by OPP is determined via community-driven indications of high priority areas, followed by external merit review of proposals. To address the evolving frontier, in FY 2012, OPP will continue and further develop its emphasis on climate change research and education, a topic of clear interest and importance to researchers and policy-makers.[14]

Regarding the $112.94 million requested for ARC for FY2012, NSF states that

> The Division of Arctic Sciences [requested FY2012] investments include: the new Discovery and Understanding in Polar Oceans, focusing on ocean circulation and including as a key component studies related to ocean acidification; the NSF-wide Science, Engineering and Education for Sustainability (SEES), creating new networks to link research teams who are exploring the human-environment nexus in a region that is experiencing rapid environmental change and on networks studying the role of clean energy in sustainability; and the NSF-wide Cyber-Infrastructure Framework for the 21st Century (CIF21), creating data management approaches that support access and archive requirements and interoperability

---

[13] National Science Foundation, *FY 2012 Budget Request to Congress*, February 14, 2011, p. OPP-1 (pdf page 175 of 468). The document is available online at http://www.nsf.gov/about/budget/fy2012/pdf/fy2012_rollup.pdf.

[14] National Science Foundation, *FY 2012 Budget Request to Congress*, February 14, 2011, pp . OPP-1 - OPP-2 (pdf pages 175-176 of 468).

among different databases. Also included are investments to enhance the efficiency, safety, and environmental footprint of activities at Summit Station in Greenland....

Arctic Sciences is organized into several programs that support research in social science, earth system science, and a broad range of natural science. Educational projects are also supported. The Research Support & Logistics program assists researchers with access to the Arctic, improves safety and environmental stewardship, and increases the ability of researchers to share plans and results with local Arctic communities. The Arctic is at the forefront of global climate change. Observations have revealed an estimated 14 percent per decade reduction in sea ice extent in the Arctic over the past 30 years, and significant summer melting of the Greenland Ice Sheet. These and many other phenomena are forcing change and uncertainty in traditional Arctic populations, present challenges and opportunities for industry and commerce, and have the potential to affect the global population through changes in sea level and changed weather patterns. Arctic Sciences funds a broad range of activities to provide an integrated understanding of environmental change in the Arctic, including study of significant, system-scale environmental change and its human dimension.[15]

January 2009 Arctic Policy Directive (NSPD 66/HSPD 25)

On January 12, 2009, the George W. Bush Administration released a presidential directive establishing a new U.S. policy for the Arctic region. The directive, dated January 9, 2009, was issued as National Security Presidential Directive 66/Homeland Security Presidential Directive 25 (NSPD 66/HSPD 25). The directive was the result of an interagency review, and it superseded for the Arctic (but not the Antarctic) a 1994 presidential directive on Arctic and Antarctic policy. The directive, among other things,

- states that the United States is an Arctic nation, with varied and compelling interests in the region;

- sets forth a six-element overall U.S. policy for the region;

- describes U.S. national security and homeland security interests in the Arctic; and

- discusses a number of issues as they relate to the Arctic, including international governance; the extended continental shelf and boundary issues; promotion of international scientific cooperation; maritime transportation; economic issues, including energy; and environmental protection and conservation of natural resources.

The Obama Administration has not issued a new directive superseding NSPD 66/HSPD 25; it is currently operating under the Bush Administration's policy directive.[16] For the text of NSPD 66/HSPD 25, see **Appendix C**.

---

[15] National Science Foundation, *FY 2012 Budget Request to Congress*, February 14, 2011, pp. OPP-2 and OPP-9 (pdf pages 176 and 183 of 468).

[16] CRS communication with State Department official, October 8, 2010.

May 2010 National Security Strategy

In May 2010, the Obama Administration released a national security strategy document, which states:

> The United States is an Arctic Nation with broad and fundamental interests in the Arctic region, where we seek to meet our national security needs, protect the environment, responsibly manage resources, account for indigenous communities, support scientific research, and strengthen international cooperation on a wide range of issues.[17]

The Arctic and the U.N. Convention on Law of the Sea (UNCLOS)[18]

Background to UNCLOS

In November 1994, the United Nations Convention on the Law of the Sea (UNCLOS) entered into force. This convention establishes a treaty regime to govern activities on, over, and under the world's oceans. It builds on the four 1958 law of the sea conventions and sets forth a framework for future activities in parts of the oceans that are beyond national jurisdiction.[19] The 1982 Convention and its 1994 Agreement relating to Implementation of Part XI of the Convention were transmitted to the Senate on October 6, 1994.[20] In the absence of Senate advice and consent to adherence, the United States is not a party to the convention and agreement.

Part VI of UNCLOS and Commission on Limits of Continental Shelf

Part VI of the convention, dealing with the Continental Shelf, and Annex II, which established a Commission on the Limits of the Continental Shelf, are most pertinent to the Arctic as it becomes more accessible ocean space, bordered by five coastal states.[21] The convention gives the coastal state sovereign jurisdiction over the resources, including oil and gas, of its continental shelf.[22] Under Article 76 of the convention, a coastal state with a broad continental margin may establish a shelf limit beyond 200 nautical miles. This jurisdiction is subject to the submission of the particulars of the intended limit and supporting scientific and technical data by the coastal state to

---

[17] *National Security Strategy*, Washington, May 2010, p. 50. The quoted sentence constitutes the entirety of the document's comments specifically on the Arctic. It is the final sentence of a section on "sustain[ing] broad cooperation on key global challenges" that includes longer discussions on climate change, peacekeeping and armed conflict, pandemics and infectious disease, transnational criminal threats and threats to governance, and safeguarding the global commons.

[18] This section prepared by Marjorie Ann Browne, Specialist in International Relations, Foreign Affairs, Defense, and Trade Division.

[19] The United States is party to the four conventions adopted in 1958: Convention on the Territorial Sea and the Contiguous Zone, Convention on the High Seas, Convention on the Continental Shelf, and Convention on Fishing and Conservation of the Living Resources of the High Seas.

[20] Treaty Document 103-39.

[21] Other relevant provisions of the Convention, applicable depending on the extent of Arctic melting, relate to navigation, high seas freedoms, fisheries, and exclusive economic zones.

[22] The continental shelf is the under-sea extension of a coastal state's land territory. Article 76 of the Convention defines the continental shelf, *inter alia*, as "the seabed and subsoil of the submarine areas that extend beyond its [coastal state's] territorial sea throughout the natural prolongation of its land territory to the outer edge of the continental margin."

---

the commission for review and recommendation.[23] The commission reviews the documentation and, by a two-thirds majority, approves its recommendations to the submitting state. Coastal states agree to establish the outer limits of their continental shelf, in accordance with this process and with their national laws. In instances of disagreement with the commission's recommendations, the coastal state may make a revised or new submission. The actions of the commission "shall not prejudice matters relating to delimitation of boundaries between States with opposite or adjacent coasts."[24] The "limits established by a coastal State on the basis of these recommendations shall be final and binding."[25]

U.S. Activities As a Non-Party to UNCLOS

As a non-party to the convention, the United States cannot participate as a member of the commission; it cannot submit a claim under Article 76. Over the years, however, it has submitted observations on submissions made by other states, requesting that those observations be made available online and to the commission. In addition, since 2001, the United States has gathered and analyzed data to determine the outer limits of its extended continental shelf. Starting in 2007, this effort became the Extended Continental Shelf Project, directed by an interagency task force under the lead of the Department of State.[26]

Some observers have suggested that a separate regime be negotiated to address the changing circumstances in the Arctic. They maintain that this phenomenon was not envisioned at the time the Law of the Sea Convention was negotiated. Still others suggest that the Arctic region above a certain parallel be designated a wilderness area, and they cite as precedent Article 4 of The Antarctic Treaty, under which any current claims to sovereign territory are frozen and

> No acts or activities taking place while the present Treaty is in force shall constitute a basis for asserting, supporting or denying a claim to territorial sovereignty in Antarctica or create any rights of sovereignty in Antarctica. No new claim, or enlargement of an existing claim, to territorial sovereignty in Antarctica shall be asserted while the present Treaty is in force.

Supporters of the Law of the Sea Convention maintain that changing circumstances in the Arctic strengthen their argument that the United States should become a party to the convention. In this way, they argue, the United States can be best situated to protect and serve its national interests, under both Article 76 and other parts of the convention.

---

[23] A coastal State party has 10 years from the entry into force of the Convention for submission of information on its proposed limits. In May 2001, the Meeting of States Parties to the Convention decided that for any State for which the Convention entered into force before May 13, 1999, the date of commencement of the 10-year time period for making submissions to the Commission is May 13, 1999.

[24] Annex II, Article 9. Article 83 of the Convention provides that questions relating to these boundary delimitation disputes shall be resolved by agreement between the States or by the Dispute Settlement options set forth in Part XV of the Convention.

[25] Article 76, para. 8.

[26] For more information, see http://www.state.gov/g/oes/continentalshelf/index.htm.

Issues for Congress

Climate Change and Loss of Arctic Sea Ice[27]

Record low extent of Arctic sea ice in 2007 focused scientific and policy attention on its linkage to global climate change, and to the implications of projected ice-free[28] seasons in the Arctic within decades. The Arctic has been projected by several scientists to be ice-free in the late summer in most years as soon as the late 2030s.[29] This opens opportunities for transport through the Northwest Passage and the Northern Sea Route, extraction of potential oil and gas resources, and expanded fishing and tourism (**Figure 3**). Loss of Arctic sea ice could also impact traditional livelihoods and cultures in the region and survival of polar bear and other animal populations, and raise risks of pollution, food supply, safety, and national security.

Like the rest of the globe, temperatures in the Arctic have varied over the past century, but show a significant warming trend, especially since the 1970s.[30] The annual average temperature for the Arctic region (from 60° to 90° N) is now about 1.8° F warmer than the average for the "climate normal" (the average from 1961 to 1990). Temperatures in October-November are now about 9° F above the seasonal normal. Scientists have concluded that most of the global warming of the last three decades is very likely caused by human-related emissions of greenhouse gases (GHG, mostly carbon dioxide); they expect the GHG-induced warming to continue for decades, even if, and after, GHG concentrations in the atmosphere have been stabilized.

Modeling of GHG-induced climate change is particularly challenging for the Arctic, but it consistently projects warming through the 21st century, with annual average Arctic temperature increases ranging from +1° to +9.0° C (+2° to +19.0° F), depending on the GHG scenario and model used. While such warming is projected by most models throughout the Arctic, some models project slight cooling localized in the North Atlantic Ocean just south of Greenland and

---

[27] This section prepared by Jane Leggett, Specialist in Energy and Environmental Policy, Resources, Science, and Industry Division.

[28] In scientific analyses, "ice-free" does not necessarily mean "no ice." The definition of "ice-free" or sea ice "extent" or "area" varies across studies. Sea ice "extent" is one common measure, equal to the sum of the area of grid cells that have less than a set percentage—frequently 15%—ice concentration. For more information, see the National Snow and Ice Data Center, http://nsidc.org/seaice/data/terminology.html.

[29] Muyin Wang and James E. Overland, "A Sea Ice Free Summer Arctic within 30 Years?," *Geophysical Research Letters* 36, no. L07502 (April 3, 2009): 10.1029/2009GL037820; Marika Holland, Cecilia M. Bitz, and Bruno Tremblay, "Future abrupt reductions in the summer Arctic sea ice," *Geophysical Research Letters* 33, no. L23503 (2006), http://www.cgd.ucar.edu/oce/mholland/abrupt_ice/holland_etal.pdf; David Adam, "Ice-free Arctic could be here in 23 years," *The Guardian*, September 5, 2007, http://www.guardian.co.uk/environment/2007/sep/05/climatechange.sciencenews. But see also Julien Boé, Alex Hall, and Xin Qu, "Sources of spread in simulations of Arctic sea ice loss over the twenty-first century," *Climatic Change* 99, no. 3 (April 1, 2010): 637-645; Wieslaw Maslowski, "Toward Advanced Modeling and Prediction of Arctic Sea Ice and Climate," in 2010 AAAS Annual Meeting, Session 1505, Toward Advanced Modeling and Prediction of Arctic Sea Ice and Climate, San Diego CA, February 19, 2010, http://aaas.confex.com/aaas/2010/webprogram/Paper1505.html; I. Eisenman and J. S. Wettlaufer, "Nonlinear threshold behavior during the loss of Arctic sea ice," *Proceedings of the National Academy of Sciences* 106, no. 1 (January 6, 2009): 28-32; Dirk Notz, "The Future of Ice Sheets and Sea Ice: Between Reversible Retreat and Unstoppable Loss," *Proceedings of the National Academy of Sciences* 106, no. 49 (December 8, 2009): 20590-20595.

[30] There was a regionally warm period in the Arctic from the mid-1920s to around 1940, which scientists have assessed to have been driven by natural climate variability. They have found that period to be distinctly different from the recent multi-decadal warming, in part because the current warmth is global.

Iceland. Most warming would occur in autumn and winter, "with very little temperature change projected over the Arctic Ocean" in summer months.[31]

The observed warmer temperatures in the Arctic have reduced sea ice extent and thickness, and the amount of ice that persists year-round ("perennial ice"); natural climate variability has likely contributed as well, such as in the record low ice extent of 2007. The 2007 record minimum sea ice extent was influenced by warm Arctic temperatures and warm, moist winds blowing from the North Pacific into the central Arctic, contributing to melting and pushing ice toward and into the Atlantic past Greenland. Warm winds did not account for the near-record sea ice minimum in 2008.[32]

Due to observed and projected climate change, scientists have concluded that the Arctic will have changed from an ice-covered environment to a recurrent ice-free[33] ocean (in summers) as soon as the late 2030s. The character of ice cover is expected to change as well, with the ice being thinner and more fragile. The variability from year to year of both ice quantity and location could be expected to continue.

---

[31] William L. Chapman and John E. Walsh, "Simulations of Arctic Temperature and Pressure by Global Coupled Models," *Journal of Climate* 20, no. 4 (February 1, 2007): 609-632.

[32] J. Overland, J. Walsh, and M. Wang, *Arctic Report Card - Atmosphere* (NOAA Arctic Research Program, October 6, 2008), http://www.arctic.noaa.gov/reportcard/atmosphere.html.

[33] See footnote 28. Also, although one Canadian scientist has predicted that recurrent ice-free summers may begin sometime between 2013 and 2020, this is not consistent with other climate models' projections.

Figure 3. Arctic Sea Ice Extent in September 2008, Compared with Prospective Shipping Routes and Oil and Gas Resources

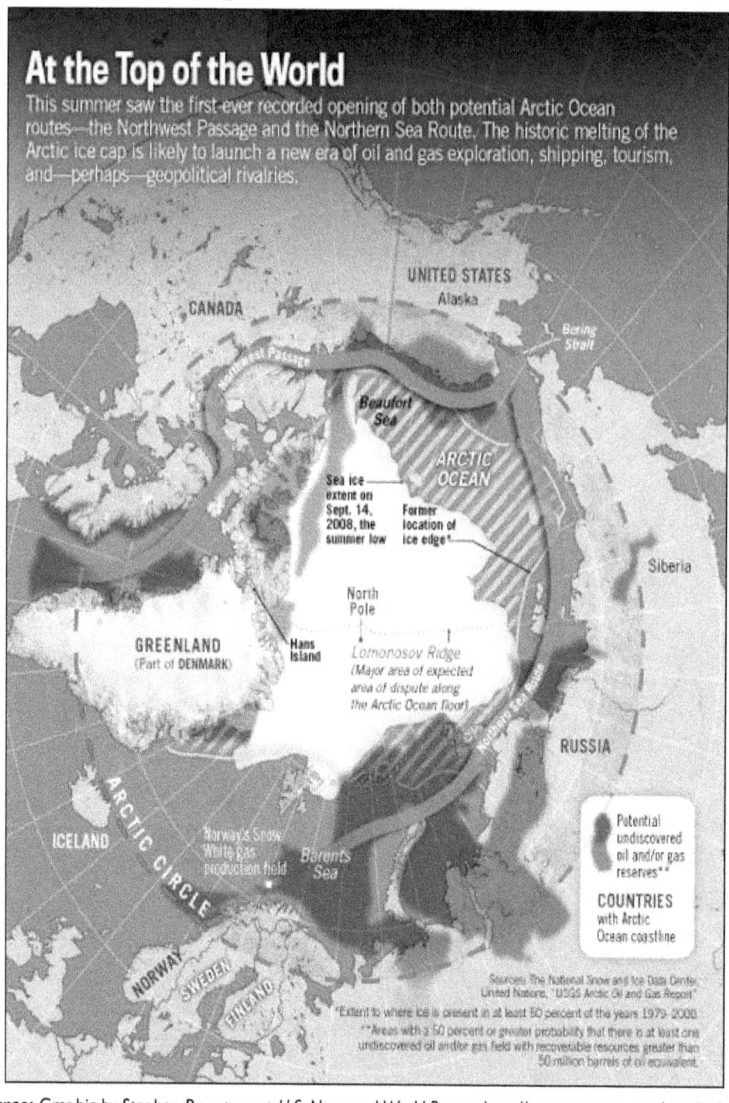

Source: Graphic by Stephen Rountree at *U.S. News and World Report,* http://www.usnews.com/articles/news/world/2008/10/09/global-warming-triggers-an-international-race-for-the-artic/photos/#1.

Territorial Claims and Sovereignty Issues[34]

Motivated in part by a desire to exercise sovereign control over the Arctic region's increasingly accessible oil and gas reserves (see "Oil, Gas, and Mineral Exploration"), the four Arctic coastal states other than the United States—Canada, Russia, Norway, and Denmark (of which Greenland is a territory)—are in the process of preparing territorial claims in the Arctic, including claims for expanded Exclusive Economic Zones (EEZs), for submission to the Commission on the Limits of the Continental Shelf. (As mentioned earlier—see "U.S. Activities As a Non-Party to UNCLOS"—the United States, as a non-party to UNCLOS, cannot participate as a member of the commission; it cannot submit a claim under Article 76. Over the years, however, it has submitted observations on submissions made by other states, requesting that those observations be made available online and to the commission. In addition, since 2001, the United States has gathered and analyzed data to determine the outer limits of its extended continental shelf.)

Russia has been attempting to chart the Arctic Ocean's enormous underwater Lomonosov Ridge in an attempt to show that it is an extension of Russia's continental margin. The Russian claim to this ridge, if accepted, would reportedly grant Russia nearly one-half of the Arctic area; a 2001 claim submitted by Russia was rejected as insufficiently documented. Canada also claims a portion of the Lomonosov Ridge as part of its own underwater continental shelf.[35] In August 2007, a Russian submersible on a research expedition deposited an encased Russian Federation flag on the seabed of the presumed site of the North Pole. The action captured worldwide attention, but analysts note that it did not constitute an official claim to the territory and was therefore a purely symbolic act.

At a May 2008 meeting in Ilulissat, Greenland, the five Arctic coastal states reaffirmed their commitment to the UNCLOS legal framework for the establishment of extended continental shelf limits in the Arctic.[36] (For further discussion, see "Extent of the Continental Margin" in "Oil, Gas, and Mineral Exploration.")

In addition to this process, there are four unresolved Arctic territorial disputes:

- Scientists have forecast that in coming decades, global warming will reduce the ice pack in Canada's northern archipelago sufficiently to permit ships to use the trans-Arctic shipping route known as the Northwest Passage during the summer months (see "Commercial Sea Transportation"). The prospect of such traffic raises a major jurisdictional question. Ottawa maintains that such a passage would be an inland waterway, and would therefore be sovereign Canadian territory subject to Ottawa's surveillance, regulation, and control. The United States, the European Union, and others assert that the passage would constitute an international strait between two high seas.

- The United States and Canada are negotiating over a binational boundary in the Beaufort Sea.

---

[34] This section prepared by Carl Ek, Specialist in International Relations, Foreign Affairs, Defense, and Trade Division.

[35] "Russia, Canada Make Competing Claims To Arctic Resources," *The Canadian Press*, September 16, 2010.

[36] "5 Countries Agree To Talk, Not Compete, Over the Arctic," *New York Times*, May 29, 2008.

- The United States and Russia in 1990 signed an agreement regarding a disputed area of the Bering Sea; the U.S. Senate ratified the pact the following year, but the Russian *Duma* has yet to approve the accord.

- Denmark and Canada disagree over which country has the territorial right to Hans Island, a tiny, barren piece of rock between Greenland and Canada's Ellesmere Island. Some analysts believe the two countries are vying for control over a future sea lane that might be created if the Arctic ice were to melt sufficiently to create a Northwest Passage. Others claim that the governments are staking out territorial claims in the event that future natural resource discoveries make the region economically valuable.[37]

In addition to these disputes, Norway and Russia had been at odds for decades over the boundary between the two in the so-called "Grey Zone" in the Barents Sea, an area believed to hold rich undersea deposits of petroleum. On September 15, 2010, Norwegian Prime Minister Jens Stoltenberg and Russian President Dmitry Medvedev signed an agreement in Murmansk, a Russian city near the Norwegian border. The accord awards roughly half of the 175,000-square-kilometer area to each country; it spells out fishing rights, and provides for the joint development of future oil and gas finds that straddle the boundary line. Some observers believe it is noteworthy that Russia would concede sovereignty over such a large, resource-rich territory to a small, neighboring country. But others have noted that Moscow may be hoping for Norwegian cooperation in developing offshore resources, and eventually in winning approval when Russia submits its Article 76 UNCLOS claim.[38]

In August 2010, Canadian Foreign Minister Lawrence Cannon announced a new "Statement of Canada's Arctic Policy," which reaffirmed the government's commitment to Canada's sovereignty in the region, to economic and social development, to environmental protection, and to empowerment of the peoples in the north. The statement also emphasized the government's intention to negotiate settlements to its disputes with the United States over the Beaufort Sea boundary, and with Denmark over Hans Island. Minister Cannon declared that "making progress on outstanding boundary issues will be a top priority."[39] Also, despite their dispute over Hans Island, Canada and Denmark have been working together on Arctic issues. In May 2010, the two countries' military chiefs of staffs signed a memorandum of understanding on Arctic Defense, Security, and Operational Cooperation, committing the two countries to "enhanced consultation, information exchange, visits, and exercises."[40]

---

[37] For additional information, see Natalie Mychajlyszyn, *The Arctic: Geopolitical Issues*, Canadian Library of Parliament, October 24, 2008.

[38] "Russia, Norway Sign Deal On Barents Sea Border, Seek More Development in Mineral-rich Arctic," *Associated Press*, September 15, 2010.

[39] Cannon quoted in "Canada Seeks To Settle Arctic Borders," *Agence France Presse*, August 20, 2010. For additional information concerning Canada's August statement on Arctic policy, see "Statement on Canada's Arctic foreign policy: Exercising sovereignty and promoting Canada's Northern Strategy abroad," Foreign Affairs and International Trade Canada website, http://www.international.gc.ca/polar-polaire/canada_arctic_foreign_policy-la_politique_etrangere_du_canada_pour_arctique.aspx?lang=eng.

[40] "Canada and Denmark Sign Arctic Cooperation Arrangement," *Targeted News Service*, May 17, 2010.

Commercial Sea Transportation[41]

Background

The search for a shorter route from the Atlantic to Asia has been the quest of maritime powers since the Middle Ages. The melting of Arctic ice raises the possibility of saving several thousands of miles and several days of sailing between major trading blocs.[42] If the Arctic were to become a viable shipping route, the ramifications could extend far beyond the Arctic. For example, lower shipping costs could be advantageous for China (at least its northeast region), Japan, and South Korea because their manufactured products exported to Europe or North America could become less expensive relative to other emerging manufacturing centers in Southeast Asia, such as India.[43] Melting ice could potentially open up two trans-Arctic routes (see **Figure 3**):[44]

- **The Northern Sea Route** (NSR, a.k.a. the "Northeast Passage"), along Russia's northern border from Murmansk to Provideniya, is about 2,600 nautical miles in length. It was opened by the Soviet Union to domestic shipping in 1931 and to transit by foreign vessels in 1991. Even so, these waters are little used by non-Russian ships.[45] This route would be applicable for trade between northeast Asia (north of Singapore) and northern Europe.

- **The Northwest Passage** (NWP) runs through the Canadian Arctic Islands. The NWP actually consists of several potential routes. The southern route is through Peel Sound in Nunavut, which has been open in recent summers and contains mostly one-year ice. However, this route is circuitous, contains some narrow channels, and is shallow enough to impose draft restrictions on ships. The more northern route, through McClure Strait from Baffin Bay to the Beaufort Sea north of Alaska, is much more direct, and therefore more appealing to ocean carriers, but more prone to ice blockage.[46] The NWP is potentially applicable for trade between northeast Asia (north of Shanghai) and the northeast of North America, but may be less commercially viable than the NSR.[47]

---

[41] This section prepared by John Frittelli, Specialist in Transportation Policy, Resources, Science, and Industry Division.

[42] Extended daylight hours in the Arctic during the summer may also be an advantage.

[43] Presentation by Stephen Carmel, Senior Vice President, Maersk Line Ltd., Halifax International Security Forum, *Arctic Security: The New Great Game?* November 21, 2009, available at http://fora.tv/.

[44] A third but more remote possibility is a route directly over the North Pole.

[45] In the summer of 2009, two German-owned ships are believed to be the first non-Russian ships to transit the NSR, sailing from Korea to deliver oil-service equipment to the Russian Arctic and then sailing on to Rotterdam.

[46] This was the route pioneered by the *SS Manhattan*, an oil tanker modified for ice breaking in 1969 to carry Alaskan North Slope oil to the Atlantic. This was the first commercial passage through the NWP, but the building of the Alaskan pipeline was found to be the more economical means of transporting oil from the North Slope to the lower 48 states.

[47] Although the NWP is often compared to the alternative route through the Panama Canal in terms of distance and sailing days from Asia to the U.S. east coast, another alternative to consider is the shorter and faster transcontinental rail route across Canada or the United States. The Panama Canal is undergoing an expansion project, expected to be completed by 2015, to allow larger ships with about three times the cargo capacity to pass through.

Destination Traffic, Not Trans-Arctic Traffic

Almost all cargo ship activity currently taking place in the Arctic is to transport natural resources from the Arctic or to deliver general cargo and supplies to communities and natural resource extraction facilities. Thus, cargo ship traffic in the Arctic presently is mostly regional, not trans-Arctic. While there has been a recent uptick in Arctic shipping activity, this activity has more to do with a spike in commodity prices than it does with the melting of Arctic ice. Even so, recent activity is less than it has been in the past. The NSR continues to account for the bulk of Arctic shipping activity. The western end of the NSR, in the Barents Sea, is open year round. Further east, sections of the NSR are open for as little as two and a half months during the summer. However, in 2011, the route was open for five months and 34 ships, accompanied by a Russian icebreaker, passed through.[48]

Cruise Ship Activity

Considerable cruise ship activity takes place in Arctic waters. In the summer of 2007, three cruise ships reportedly sailed through the NWP from the Atlantic to Alaska's North Slope.[49] In August 2010, a cruise ship with over 150 passengers ran aground in the NWP. In the Barents Sea, there are regular cruise ships sailing to Svalbard. The inherent dangers for passenger ships in the Arctic have prompted calls for international regulations promoting the safety of cruise ships in the area. Some have suggested that cruise ships sail in pairs to provide assistance to one another, given the Arctic's remoteness and the difficulty land-based rescuers would have in reaching a vessel in distress.[50] Requiring that Arctic cruise vessels have ice-strengthened hulls and be equipped with enclosed lifeboats could be other safety requirements. In 2003, some Arctic cruise and tourist operators formed the Association of Arctic Expedition Cruise Operators (AECO) to establish agreed-upon safety and environmental protection guidelines, but this organization only covers the portion of the Arctic around Greenland, Svalbard, and Jan Mayen.[51]

Unpredictable Ice Conditions Hinder Trans-Arctic Shipping

Arctic waters do not necessarily have to be ice free to be open to shipping. Multiyear ice can be over 10 feet thick and problematic even for icebreakers, but one-year ice is typically 3 feet thick or less. This thinner ice can be more readily broken up by icebreakers or ice class ships (cargo ships with reinforced hulls and other features for navigating in ice-infested waters). However, more open water in the Arctic has resulted in another potential obstacle to shipping: unpredictable ice flows. In the NWP, melting ice and the opening of waters that were once covered with one-year ice has allowed blocks of multiyear ice from farther north, or icebergs from Greenland, to flow into potential sea lanes. The source of this multiyear ice is not predicted to dissipate in spite of climate change. Moreover, the flow patterns of these ice blocks are very difficult to predict, and they have floated into potential routes for shipping.[52] Thus, the lack of ice in potential sea lanes during the summer months can add even greater unpredictability to Arctic shipping. This is

---

[48] ITAR-TASS, "Rosatomflot Ends Shipping Season Along Northern Sea Route," November 29, 2011.

[49] "U.S. Needs to Prepare for Arctic Traffic Surge," *Anchorage Daily News*, February 12, 2008, p. A4.

[50] "Northern Waters," *The Globe and Mail* (Canada), August 14, 2008, p. A8.

[51] See http://www.aeco.no/index.htm for more information.

[52] S.E.L. Howell and J.J. Yackel, "A Vessel Transit Assessment of Sea Ice Variability in the Western Arctic, 1969-2002: Implications for Ship Navigation," *Canadian Journal of Remote Sensing*, vol. 30, no. 2, 2004.

---

in addition to the extent of ice versus open water, which is also highly variable from one year to the next and seasonally.

The unpredictability of ice conditions is a major hindrance for trans-Arctic shipping in general, but can be more of a concern for some types of ships than it is for others. For instance, it would be less of a concern for cruise ships, which may have the objective of merely visiting the Arctic rather than passing through and could change their route and itinerary depending on ice conditions. On the other hand, unpredictability is of the utmost concern for container ships that carry thousands of containers from hundreds of different customers, all of whom expect to unload or load their cargo upon the ship's arrival at various ports as indicated on the ship's advertised schedule. The presence of even small blocks of ice or icebergs from a melting Greenland ice sheet requires slow sailing and could play havoc with schedules. Ships carrying a single commodity in bulk from one port to another for just one customer have more flexibility in terms of delivery windows, but would not likely risk an Arctic passage under prevailing conditions.

Ice is not the sole impediment to Arctic shipping. The region frequently experiences adverse weather, including not only severe storms, but also intense cold, which can impair deck machinery. During the summer months when sea lanes are open, heavy fog is common in the Arctic.

Commercial ships would face higher operating costs on Arctic routes than elsewhere. Ship size is an important factor in reducing freight costs. Many ships currently used in other waters would require two icebreakers to break a path wide enough for them to sail through; ship owners could reduce that cost by using smaller vessels in the Arctic, but this would raise the cost per container or per ton of freight.[53] Also, icebreakers or ice-class cargo vessels burn more fuel than ships designed for more temperate waters and would have to sail at slower speeds. The shipping season in the Arctic only lasts for a few weeks, so icebreakers and other special required equipment would sit idle the remainder of the year. None of these impediments by themselves may be enough to discourage Arctic passage but they do raise costs, perhaps enough to negate the savings of a shorter route. Thus, from the perspective of a shipper or a ship owner, shorter via the Arctic does not necessarily mean cheaper and faster.[54]

Basic Navigation Infrastructure Is Lacking

Considerable investment in navigation-related infrastructure would be required if trans-Arctic shipping were to become a reality. Channel marking buoys and other floating visual aids are not possible in Arctic waters because moving ice sheets will continuously shift their positions. Therefore, vessel captains would need to rely on marine surveys and ice charts. For some areas in the Arctic, however, these surveys and charts are out of date and not sufficiently accurate.[55] To remedy this problem, aviation reconnaissance of ice conditions and satellite images would need to

---

[53] "Arctic Unlikely to See Major Shipping Growth," *New Zealand Transport and Logistics Business Week*, April 24, 2008.

[54] Presentation by Stephen Carmel, Senior Vice President, Maersk Line Ltd., Halifax International Security Forum, *Arctic Security: The New Great Game?* November 21, 2009, available at http://fora.tv/.

[55] In July and August 2010, NOAA surveyed the Bering Straits area in order to update its charts but stated that it will take more than 25 years to map the prioritized areas of navigational significance in U.S. Arctic waters. See http://www.noaanews.noaa.gov/stories2010/20100720_fairweather.html.

become readily available for ship operators.[56] Ship-to-shore communication infrastructure would need to be installed where possible. Refueling stations may be needed, as well as, perhaps, transshipment ports where cargo could be transferred to and from ice-capable vessels at both ends of Arctic routes. Shipping lines would need to develop a larger pool of mariners with ice navigation experience. Marine insurers would need to calculate the proper level of risk premium for polar routes, which would require more detailed information about Arctic accidents and incidents in the past.

The U.S. Army Corps of Engineers, along with the State of Alaska, is studying the feasibility of a "deep-draft" port in the Arctic (accommodating ships with a draft of up to 35 feet). The northern and northwestern coastlines of Alaska are exceptionally shallow, generally limiting harbor and near shore traffic to shallow-draft barges. Coast Guard cutters and icebreakers have drafts of 35 to 40 feet while NOAA research vessels have drafts of 16 to 28 feet, so at present these vessels are based outside the Arctic and must sail considerable distances to reach Arctic duty stations. Supply vessels supporting offshore oil rigs typically have drafts over 20 feet. A deep-draft port could serve as a base of operations for larger vessels, facilitating commercial maritime traffic in the Arctic.[57]

Another study on maritime infrastructure needs is being conducted by the U.S. Committee on the Marine Transportation System, a cabinet-level committee of federal agencies with responsibilities for marine transportation. It is due to report to Congress in 2012 a priority of federal actions the committee believes are needed to ensure maritime safety, environmental protection, and national security in the Arctic.[58]

Regulation of Arctic Shipping

Due to the international nature of the shipping industry, maritime trading nations have adopted international treaties that establish standards for ocean carriers in terms of safety, pollution prevention, and security. These standards are agreed upon by shipping nations through the International Maritime Organization (IMO), a United Nations agency that first met in 1959.[59]

Key conventions that the 168 IMO member nations have adopted include the Safety of Life at Sea Convention (SOLAS), which was originally adopted in response to the *Titanic* disaster in 1912 but has since been revised several times; the Prevention of Pollution from Ships (MARPOL), which was adopted in 1973 and modified in 1978; and the Standards for Training, Certification, and Watchkeeping for Seafarers (SCTW), which was adopted in 1978 and amended in 1995. It is up to ratifying nations to enforce these standards. The United States is a party to these conventions, and the U.S. Coast Guard enforces them when it boards and inspects ships and crews arriving at U.S. ports and the very few ships engaged in international trade that sail under the U.S. flag.

---

[56] Ice reporting that currently exists is intended for scientists not mariners.

[57] For further information, see http://www.poa.usace.army.mil/en/cw/AKPortsStudy.htm, and FY2013 USACE Budget Justification, p. POD-5.

58

See http://www.cmts.gov/Activities/ActionTeams.aspx

[59] See http://www.imo.org/ for more information.

Like the United States, most of the other major maritime trading nations lack the ability to enforce these regulations as a "flag state" because much of the world's merchant fleet is registered under so-called "flags of convenience." While most ship owners and operators are headquartered in developed countries, they often register their ships in Panama, Liberia, the Bahamas, the Marshall Islands, Malta, and Cyprus, among other "open registries," because these nations offer more attractive tax and employment regulatory regimes. Because of this development, most maritime trading nations enforce shipping regulations under a "port state control" regime—that is, they require compliance with these regulations as a condition of calling at their ports. The fragmented nature of ship ownership and operation can be a further hurdle to regulatory enforcement. It is common for cargo ships to be owned by one company, operated by a second company (which markets the ship's space), and managed by a third (which may supply the crew and other services a ship requires to sail), each of which could be headquartered in different countries.

Arctic Guidelines

While SOLAS and other IMO conventions include provisions regarding the operation of ships in ice-infested waters, they are not specific to the polar regions. To supplement existing requirements, in December 2002, the IMO approved guidelines for ships operating in Arctic ice-covered waters.[60] These were only recommendations for ships operating in the Arctic, not requirements. They apply to passenger and cargo ships of 500 gross tons or more engaged in international voyages. They do not apply to fishing vessels, military vessels, pleasure yachts, and smaller cargo ships. The guidelines are intended to improve safety and prevent pollution in the Arctic, and they include provisions on ship construction, ship equipment related to navigation, and crew training and ship operation. The guidelines recommend that ships carry fully enclosed lifeboats or carry tarpaulins to cover their lifeboats. They recommend that each crew include at least one ice navigator with documented evidence of having completed an ice navigation training program. The IMO is in the process of drafting mandatory requirements for ships operating in the Arctic.[61]

Nations can enforce additional requirements on ships arriving at their ports or sailing through their coastal waters. For instance, U.S. Coast Guard regulations largely follow IMO conventions but mandate additional requirements in some areas. U.S. coastal states can require ships calling at their ports to take additional safety and pollution prevention safeguards. Canada and Russia have additional pollution regulations for Arctic waters exceeding MARPOL. The U.S. Coast Guard is seeking agreement with Russia to establish a vessel traffic separation scheme for the Bering Strait between Alaska and Russia, which now experiences over 300 transits per year.[62]

---

[60] See MSC/Circ. 1056/MEPC/Circ.399 at http://www.imo.org/.

[61] Edwin H. Anderson, "Polar Shipping, The Forthcoming Polar Code and Implications for the Polar Environments," *Journal of Maritime Law and Commerce*, v. 43, no. 1, January 2012.

[62] The Coast Guard is studying shipping routes through the Bering Strait for possible safety enhancements. See 75 FR 68568, November 8, 2010.

Oil, Gas, and Mineral Exploration[63]

Changes to the Arctic brought about by warming temperatures resulting from climate change will likely allow more exploration for oil and gas offshore where the extent of summer sea ice is shrinking. Similarly, shrinking glaciers onshore could expose land containing economic deposits of gold, iron ore, or other minerals that were previously covered by glacial ice. Warming that causes permafrost to melt could also pose challenges to onshore exploration activities because ground structures, such as pipelines and other infrastructure that depend on footings sunk into the permafrost for support, could become unstable. Despite the warming temperatures, however, exploration and development in the Arctic would still be subject to harsh conditions, especially in winter, which makes it costly and challenging to develop infrastructure necessary to produce, store, and transport oil, gas, and minerals from newly discovered deposits.

Shrinking sea ice cover in the Arctic has also intensified interest in mapping the continental margins of countries with lands in the Arctic. Delineating the extent of the continental margins beyond the 200 nautical mile Exclusive Economic Zone (EEZ) under the terms of Article 76 of the U.N. Convention on the Law of the Sea (UNCLOS) could open up substantial amounts of submerged lands for development. Mapping projects are underway, by individual countries and in cooperative studies, that would be used to support national claims to submerged lands which may contain large amounts of oil, natural gas, methane hydrates, or minerals.

Expiration of the annual congressional moratoria on September 30, 2008, coupled with other developments in offshore leasing activity, impacts federal policies on Arctic offshore development in a number of ways.[64] The expiration of leasing restrictions allows Outer Continental Shelf (OCS) areas where leasing has not been considered for many years to be considered for potential federal leasing activity. Other developments in offshore leasing activity include a presidential order to lift the executive restrictions on certain OCS areas to allow offshore drilling,[65] the emergence of new offshore operations (OCS renewable energy leasing in Arctic areas[66]), and the general emergence of new technologies related to OCS research and development. Diminished leasing restrictions impact OCS activity in a domestic and an international context and generally contribute to the larger debate over OCS drilling in the Arctic.

---

[63] This section prepared by Curry Hagerty, Specialist in Energy and Natural Resources Policy, Resources, Science, and Industry Division; Peter Folger, Specialist in Energy and Natural Resources Policy, Resources, Science, and Industry Division; and Marc Humphries, Analyst in Energy Policy, Resources, Science, and Industry Division.

[64] The Continuing Appropriations Resolution 2009 (P.L. 110-329) did not extend the annual congressional moratorium on oil and gas leasing activities. On March 11, 2009, the Omnibus Appropriations Act, 2009 (P.L. 111-8) was enacted without moratoria provisions, confirming that the oil and gas development moratoria in the OCS along the Atlantic and Pacific Coasts, parts of Alaska, and the Gulf of Mexico that had been in place since 1982 had not been restored in 2009 appropriations measures. The combined effect of Presidential Directives from 1990 to 2008 also impacted moratoria constraints.

[65] On July 14, 2008, a Modification of the Presidential Withdrawal of areas of the United States Outer Continental Shelf from leasing disposition was announced by President Bush in the following statement, "Under the authority vested in me as President of the United States, including section 12(a) of the Outer Continental Shelf Lands Act, 43 U.S.C. 1341(a), I hereby modify the prior memoranda of withdrawals from disposition by leasing of the United States Outer Continental Shelf issued on August 4, 1992."

[66] Effective on June 29, 2009, the rule established two types of leases: (1) commercial leases for full development and power generation, and (2) limited leases for resource assessment and technology testing. See 73 Fed Reg 39376.

Oil and Gas

A primary driver for the increased interest in exploring for oil and gas offshore in the Arctic is the shrinking Arctic ice cap, or conversely, the growing amount of ice-free ocean in the summertime. Reduced sea ice in the summer means that ships towing seismic arrays[67] can explore previously inaccessible regions of the Arctic Ocean, Chukchi Sea, Beaufort Sea and other offshore regions for longer periods of time without risk of colliding with floating sea ice. Less sea ice over longer periods compared to previous decades also means that the seasonal window for offshore drilling in the Arctic remains open longer in the summer and increases the chances for making a discovery.

In addition to the improved access to larger portions of the Arctic afforded by shrinking sea ice, recent interest in Arctic oil and gas was fueled by a 2008 U.S. Geological Survey (USGS) appraisal of undiscovered oil and gas north of the Arctic Circle.[68] The USGS asserts that "The extensive Arctic continental shelves may constitute the geographically largest unexplored prospective area for petroleum remaining on Earth."[69] In the report, the USGS estimates that 90 billion barrels of oil, nearly 1,700 trillion cubic feet of natural gas, and 44 billion barrels of natural gas liquids may remain to be discovered in the Arctic. Nearly all (84%) of the oil and gas is expected to occur offshore. The USGS estimate for total undiscovered oil and gas in the Arctic exceeds the total discovered amount of Arctic oil and oil-equivalent natural gas (240 billion barrels), which constitutes almost 10% of the world's known conventional petroleum resources.[70] An important caveat to the USGS assessment, however, is that it excludes economic considerations. The report only includes resources that would be technically recoverable with current technology; they may not necessarily be economically recoverable under prevailing oil and gas prices.

Despite the warming trend in the Arctic, a discovery of new oil and gas deposits far from existing storage, pipelines, and shipping facilities can not be developed until infrastructure is built to extract and transport the petroleum. For example, a Devon Energy spokesman noted in April 2008 that a 240 million barrel discovery in the Beaufort Sea won't be developed for at least 10 years because the company does not have the infrastructure to transport the oil.[71] Other areas with oil and gas potential, such as offshore east Greenland, may take even longer to develop because they are still covered by substantial summer sea ice that would hinder exploration and development unless more ice melts.[72]

---

[67] A seismic array is typically a long string or streamer of geophones—acoustic devices used for recording seismic signals—towed behind a ship while the ship traverses a prospective oil and gas-bearing portion of the seafloor. The seismic signals are processed and interpreted to give a cross-section or three-dimensional image of the subsurface.

[68] See USGS Circum-Arctic Resource Appraisal website at http://energy.usgs.gov/arctic/.

[69] USGS Fact Sheet 2008-3049: Circum-Arctic Resource Appraisal: Estimates of Undiscovered Oil and Gas North of the Arctic Circle; at http://pubs.usgs.gov/fs/2008/3049/.

[70] USGS Fact Sheet 2008-3049: Circum-Arctic Resource Appraisal: Estimates of Undiscovered Oil and Gas North of the Arctic Circle; at http://pubs.usgs.gov/fs/2008/3049/.

[71] Hugo Miller, "BHP Billiton Leads Arctic Gold Hunt in Global Warming Bonanza," Bloomberg.com (April 16, 2008), at http://www.bloomberg.com/apps/news?pid=20601081&sid=ag.kQZln.mFg&refer=australia.

[72] The Associated Press, "Greenland Opens to Oil Firms; Melting Ice Unlocks Reserves," International Herald Tribune (January 14, 2008), at http://www.iht.com/articles/ap/2008/01/14/business/NA-FIN-US-Greenland-Oil-Companies.php.

Extent of the Continental Margin

Increased interest in developing offshore resources in the Arctic has sparked efforts by nations bordering the Arctic Ocean to map the extent of their continental margins beyond the 200-mile EEZ limit. Under UNCLOS, nations can submit a claim to submerged lands if they demonstrate that their continental margin extends beyond the 200-mile limit according to the definition in Article 76. Under Article 76, the extent of the continental margin beyond the 200-mile limit depends on the position of the foot of the continental slope, the thickness of sediments, and the depth of water. Also, the continental margin could include geologic features that extend from the continent out to sea, which may include undersea ridges continuing for hundreds of miles offshore.

As mentioned earlier—see "U.S. Activities As a Non-Party to UNCLOS"—the United States, as a non-party to UNCLOS, cannot participate as a member of the Commission on the Limits of the Continental Shelf; it cannot submit a claim under Article 76. Over the years, however, it has submitted observations on submissions made by other states, requesting that those observations be made available online and to the commission. In addition, since 2001, the United States has gathered and analyzed data to determine the outer limits of its extended continental shelf.

Arctic border countries have begun the complex investigations needed to support claims for an extended continental shelf in the Arctic. Claims have already been submitted by several countries, including the Russian Federation, which submitted its UNCLOS claim to a portion of the Arctic continental shelf in 2001.[73] Russia made claims to the Lomonosov Ridge, an undersea feature spanning the Arctic from Russia to Canada, as an extension of its continental margin. The submission demonstrated Russia's bid to extend activities in Arctic regions. The United States has started to gather and analyze data through an initiative called the Extended Continental Shelf Project.[74] In this effort, the United States is working closely with Canada to prepare and present Canada's submission to the Commission on the Limits of the Continental Shelf.

Canada and the United States share overlapping regions of the seabed as part of the extended continental margin of both nations. Both countries have conducted research singly and jointly to map the extended continental shelf.[75] In August 2008, Canada's prime minister announced that Canada would spend $100 million (Canadian) over five years to map its total Arctic mineral and energy resources and bolster Canada's sovereignty over its northern resources.[76] On January 12, 2009, the Bush Administration issued a presidential directive addressing the extended continental shelf and boundary issues in the Arctic, among other issues, including national security and maritime transportation.[77] The directive acknowledges an unresolved boundary between the United States and Canada in the Beaufort Sea, and notes that Russia and the United States abide

---

[73] Tony Halpin, "President Medvedev Threatens Russian Arctic Annexation," Times Online (September 18, 2008), at http://www.timesonline.co.uk/tol/news/world/europe/article4773567.ece.

[74] The purpose of the U.S. Extended Continental Shelf Project is to establish the full extent of the continental shelf of the United States, consistent with international law. Involved in this mission are the U.S. Coast Guard (USCG), Department of State (DOS), and the University of New Hampshire (UNH). NOAA has the lead in collecting bathymetric data. The U.S. Geological Survey has the lead in collecting seismic data.

[75] See USGS, U.S. Extended Continental Shelf Project, at http://www.state.gov/g/oes/continentalshelf/.

[76] Press release, Office of the Prime Minister, Canada (August 26, 2008), at http://www.pm.gc.ca/eng/media.asp?category=1&id=2242.

[77] National Security Presidential Directive/NSPD-66 and Homeland Security Presidential Directive/HSPD-25, at http://www.whitehouse.gov/news/releases/2009/01/20090112-3.html.

by a 1990 maritime boundary treaty pending its entry into force once it is ratified by the Russian Federation. According to the USGS, however, most of the potential oil and gas resources estimated for the Arctic are likely to occur within already agreed-upon territorial boundaries.[78] (For further discussion, see "Territorial Claims and Sovereignty Issues.")

Minerals

A warming Arctic means new opportunities and challenges for mineral exploration and development. Receding glaciers expose previously ice-covered land that could host economic mineral deposits that were previously undetectable and un-mineable below the ice. Longer summers would also extend exploration seasons even for areas not currently ice-covered but which are only accessible for ground surveys during the warmer months. In some parts of the Arctic, such as Baffin Island, Canada, less sea ice allows ships to transport heavy equipment to remote locations, and to convey ore from mines to the market further south. Some railway and mining operators are considering developing railroads and other infrastructure to transport ore year-round.[79] As with onshore oil and gas development, however, mining infrastructure that depends on footings sunk into permafrost could become unstable if the permafrost melts in response to warmer temperatures. Also, as with oil and gas development, mineral deposits that may be technically recoverable with current technology may not be economically profitable.

One important part of the current infrastructure in the Arctic that supports oil, gas, and mineral development is the construction and use of ice roads—built and used during the winter—but which are not passable during the warmer months. Warmer temperatures are shortening the ice road transport seasons and creating transportation challenges. For example, the opening date for tundra roads in northern Alaska has shifted from early November prior to 1991 to January in recent years.[80]

Environment and Economics

The warming Arctic has focused attention on threats to its wildlife and ecosystems, and it is expected that increased oil, gas, and mineral exploration and development activities may also invite increased scrutiny of possible harm to the fragile Arctic ecosystems. Federal offshore programs are often the subject of this type of scrutiny, as demonstrated by litigation largely focusing on environmental impacts. For example, plaintiffs in cases challenging government approval of OCS development activity in the Chukchi Sea generally are local communities and national environmental groups. The defendant in litigation over federal leasing in the Alaska program areas is the Secretary of the Interior. Typically litigation over federal offshore programs in Alaska takes place in two venues—the U.S. Court of Appeals for the Ninth Circuit, and/or the U.S. District Court of the District of Alaska. The schedule for litigation can be an issue because the schedule in one venue has some bearing on rulings related to litigation in the other venue. A

---

[78] Don Gautier, Research Geologist, USGS, quoted in "Countries in Tug-of-War Over Arctic Resources," CNN.com (January 2, 2009), at http://www.cnn.com/2009/TECH/science/01/02/arctic.rights.dispute/index.html?iref=newssearch.

[79] Carolyn Fitzpatrick, "Heavy Haul in the High North," Railway Gazette International (July 24, 2008), at http://www.railwaygazette.com/news/single-view/view/10/heavy-haul-in-the-high-north.html.

[80] See National Oceanic and Atmospheric Administration, Arctic Change, at http://www.arctic.noaa.gov/detect/land-road.shtml?page=land.

new schedule for litigation regarding OCS development in the Chukchi Sea is currently under consideration. The outcome of court cases will likely impact future development activities.

The outcome of judicial action on environmental regulations is not yet known, but it is widely accepted that complying with current environmental laws and regulations in the Arctic adds to the comparatively high cost of doing business in the far north. In addition, the price and price stability of petroleum and mineral commodities will underlie industry decisions about whether to make large investments in multi-year exploration and development projects in the Arctic. Low or volatile prices could curtail any sustained development efforts north of the Arctic Circle, even if continued warming opens new territory to petroleum and mineral exploration. In addition to uncertainty regarding the price of oil, gas, and minerals, and the environmental considerations that accompany exploration and development, there is the uncertainty for the United States regarding its claims to submerged lands beyond the 200-mile EEZ.

Even if the commodity prices and environmental costs were favorable toward exploration and development, uncertainty over U.S. claims to the extended continental shelf—because the United States is a non-party to UNCLOS—may influence private sector decisions to invest in Arctic oil, gas, and mineral resource development.

Oil Pollution and Pollution Response[81]

Oil Pollution Implications of Arctic Change

Climate change impacts in the Arctic, particularly the decline of sea ice and retreating glaciers, have stimulated human activities in the region, many of which have the potential to create oil pollution. A primary concern is the threat of a large oil spill in the area. Although a major oil spill has not occurred in the Arctic region,[82] recent economic activity, such as oil and gas exploration and tourism (cruise ships), increases the risk of oil pollution (and other kinds of pollution) in the Arctic. Significant spills in high northern latitudes (e.g., the 1989 *Exxon Valdez* spill in Alaska and spills in the North Sea) suggest that the "potential impacts of an Arctic spill are likely to be severe for Arctic species and ecosystems."[83]

Risk of Oil Pollution in the Arctic

A primary factor determining the risk of oil pollution in the Arctic is the level and type of human activity being conducted in the region. Although climate changes in the Arctic are expected to increase access to natural resources and shipping lanes, the region will continue to present logistical challenges that may hinder human activity in the region. For example (as discussed in another section of this report),[84] the unpredictable ice conditions may discourage trans-Arctic shipping. If trans-Arctic shipping were to occur on a frequent basis, it would represent a considerable portion of the overall risk of oil pollution in the region. In recent decades, many of

---

[81] This section prepared by Jonathan L. Ramseur, Specialist in Environmental Policy, Resources, Science, and Industry Division.

[82] Arctic Monitoring and Assessment Programme (AMAP), Arctic Oil and Gas 2007 (2008).

[83] Arctic Monitoring and Assessment Programme (AMAP), Arctic Oil and Gas 2007 (2008).

[84] See this report's section "Implications for Sea Transportation," by John Fritelli.

the world's largest oil spills have been from oil tankers, which can carry millions of gallons of oil.[85]

Although the level of trans-Arctic shipping is uncertain, many expect oil exploration and extraction activities to intensify in the region.[86] Oil well blowouts from offshore oil extraction operations have been a source of major oil spills, eclipsing the largest tanker spills. The largest unintentional oil spill in recent history was from the 2010 *Deepwater Horizon* incident in the Gulf of Mexico.[87] During that incident, the uncontrolled well released (over an 84-day period) approximately 200 million gallons of crude oil into the Gulf.[88] The second-largest unintentional oil spill in recent history—the *IXTOC I*, estimated at 140 million gallons—was due to an oil well blowout in Mexican Gulf Coast waters in 1979.[89]

Until the 2010 *Deepwater Horizon* incident, the spill record for offshore platforms in U.S. federal waters had shown improvement from prior years.[90] A 2003 National Research Council (NRC) study of oil and gas activities on Alaska's North Slope stated "the conclusion of these analyses is that blowouts that result in large spills are unlikely."[91] Similar conclusions were made in federal agency documents regarding deepwater drilling in the Gulf of Mexico before the 2010 *Deepwater Horizon* event.[92] Some would likely contend that the underlying analyses behind these conclusions should be adjusted to account for the 2010 Gulf oil spill. However, others may argue that the proposed activities in U.S. Arctic waters present less risk of an oil well blowout than was encountered by the *Deepwater Horizon* drill rig, because the proposed U.S. Arctic operations would be in shallower waters (150 feet) than the deepwater well (approximately 5,000 feet) that was involved in the 2010 Gulf oil spill. In addition, Shell Oil has stated that the pressures in the Chukchi Sea (the location of Shell's recent interest) would be two to three times less than they were in well involved in the 2010 Gulf oil spill.[93] Regardless of these differences, even under the most stringent control systems, some oil spills and other accidents are likely to occur from equipment failure or human error.

---

[85] For example, the *Exxon Valdez* spilled approximately 11 million gallons of oil, but its carrying capacity was approximately 60 million gallons.

[86] See this report's section "Implication of Changes in the Arctic for Oil, Gas, and Mineral Exploration and Development," by Peter Folger and Marc Humphries.

[87] Larger oil spills occurred during the 1991 Iraq War, but many of those spills were deliberate. A 1910-1911 onshore oil blowout in the California San Joaquin Valley is reported to have spilled 9.4 million barrels of crude oil (almost 400 million gallons).

[88] See CRS Report R41531, *Deepwater Horizon Oil Spill: The Fate of the Oil*, by Jonathan L. Ramseur.

[89] National Research Council (NRC) of the National Academies of Science, *Oil in the Sea III: Inputs, Fates, and Effects* (2003).

[90] See CRS Report RL33705, *Oil Spills in U.S. Coastal Waters: Background and Governance*, by Jonathan L. Ramseur; and Dagmar Etkin (Environmental Research Consulting), Analysis of U.S. Oil Spillage, Prepared for American Petroleum Institute, August 2009.

[91] National Research Council of the National Academies of Science, *Cumulative Environmental Effects of Oil and Gas Activities on Alaska's North Slope* (2003).

[92] See, for example, Minerals Management Service (MMS), Outer Continental Shelf Oil & Gas Leasing Program: 2007-2012, Final Environmental Impact Statement, April 2007, Chapter 4; MMS, Proposed Gulf of Mexico OCS Oil and Gas Lease Sale 206, Central Planning Area, Environmental Assessment, October 2007;

[93] Letter from Marvin E. Odum, President, Shell Oil Company to S. Elizabeth Birnbaum, Minerals Management Service (May 14, 2010). Cited in a staff paper from the National Commission on the BP Deepwater Horizon Oil Spill and Offshore Drilling ("The Challenges of Oil Spill Response in the Arctic," January 2011).

Potential Impacts

No oil spill is entirely benign. Even a relatively minor spill, depending on the timing and location, can cause significant harm to individual organisms and entire populations. Regarding aquatic spills, marine mammals, birds, bottom-dwelling and intertidal species, and organisms in early developmental stages—eggs or larvae—are especially vulnerable. However, the effects of oil spills can vary greatly. Oil spills can cause impacts over a range of time scales, from only a few days to several years, or even decades in some cases.

Conditions in the Arctic may have implications for toxicological effects that are not yet understood. For example, oil spills on permafrost may persist in an ecosystem for relatively long periods of time, potentially harming plant life through their root systems. Moreover, little is known about the effects of oil spills on species that are unique to the Arctic, particularly, species' abilities to thrive in a cold environment and the effect temperature has on toxicity.[94]

The effects of oil spills in high latitude, cold ocean environments may last longer and cause greater damage than expected. Some recent studies have found that oil spills in lower latitudes have persisted for longer than initially expected, thus raising the concern that the persistence of oil in the Arctic may be understated. In terms of wildlife, population recovery may take longer in the Arctic because many of the species have longer life spans and reproduce at a slower rate.[95]

Response and Cleanup Challenges in the Arctic Region

Climate changes in the Arctic are expected to increase human activities in the region, many of which impose a risk of oil pollution, particularly from oil spills. Conditions in the Arctic region impose unique challenges for personnel charged with (1) oil spill response, the process of getting people and equipment to the incident, and (2) cleanup duties, either recovering the spilled oil or mitigating the contamination so that it poses less harm to the ecosystem. These challenges may play a role in the policy development for economic activities in the Arctic.

Spill Response Challenges

Response time is a critical factor for oil spill recovery. With each hour, spilled oil becomes more difficult to track, contain, and recover, particularly in icy conditions, where oil can migrate under or mix with surrounding ice.[96] Most response techniques call for quick action, which may pose logistical challenges in areas without prior staging equipment or trained response professionals. Many stakeholders are concerned about a "response gap" for oil spills in the Arctic region.[97] A response gap is a period of time in which oil spill response activities would be unsafe or infeasible. The response gap for the northern Arctic latitudes is likely to be extremely high compared to other regions.[98]

---

[94] AMAP, *Arctic Oil and Gas 2007 (2008)*.

[95] AMAP, *Arctic Oil and Gas 2007* (2008).

[96] World Wildlife Fund, *Oil Spill: Response Challenges in Arctic Waters* (2007).

[97] Coastal Response Research Center, *Opening the Arctic Seas: Envisioning Disasters and Framing Solutions* (2009), partnership between the National Oceanic and Atmospheric Administration and the University of New Hampshire.

[98] Although the response gap in the Arctic has not been quantified, a recent estimate of Prince William Sound (PWS) may be instructive. A 2007 study found a response gap for PWS of 38% for the time of the study period (65% during (continued...)

According to the former Commander of the 17th Coast Guard District (Alaska), "we are not prepared for a major oil spill [over 100,000 gallons] in the Arctic environment. The Coast Guard has no offshore response capability in Northern or Western Alaska."[99] The transportation infrastructure along Alaska's northern coast poses challenges for oil spill responders. The Coast Guard has no designated air stations north of Kodiak, AK, which is almost 1,000 miles from the northernmost point of land along the Alaskan coast in Point Barrow, AK.[100] Although some of communities have airstrips capable of landing cargo planes, no roads connect these communities.[101] Vessel infrastructure is also limited. The nearest major port is in the Aleutian Islands, approximately 1,300 miles from Point Barrow. A 2010 Government Accountability Office (GAO) report identified further logistical obstacles that would hinder an oil spill response in the region, including "inadequate" ocean and weather information for the Arctic and technological problems with communications.[102]

The history of oil spills and response in the Aleutian Islands raises concerns for potential spills in the Arctic region:

> The past 20 years of data on response to spills in the Aleutians has also shown that almost no oil has been recovered during events where attempts have been made by the responsible parties or government agencies, and that in many cases, weather and other conditions have prevented any response at all.[103]

Oil Spill Cleanup Challenges

The behavior of oil spills in cold and icy waters is not well understood.[104] Cleaning up oil spills in ice-covered waters will be more difficult than in other areas, primarily because effective strategies have yet to be developed. Natural oil seeps, which are a major source of oil in the arctic environment, may offer opportunities for studying the behavior of oil.[105]

The Arctic conditions present several hurdles to oil cleanup efforts. In colder water temperatures, there are fewer organisms to break down the oil through microbial degradation. Oil evaporates at

---

(...continued)

the winter season). Note that PWS has existing infrastructure for response, while the more remote Arctic areas do not. Nuka Research and Planning Group, LLC, *Response Gap Estimate for Two Operating Areas in Prince William Sound, Alaska* (2007), Report to Prince William Sound Regional Citizens' Advisory Council.

[99] Arthur Brooks (Commander, 17th Coast Guard District) Coast Guard Journal, Arctic Journal (April 7, 2008).

[100] U.S. Coast Guard, *Report to Congress: U.S. Coast Guard Polar Operations*, December 2008.

[101] A single road connects Deadhorse, Alaska and the Prudhoe Bay with central Alaska (Fairbanks). For more details and maps of the area, see Nuka Research and Planning Group, *Oil Spill Prevention and Response in the U.S. Arctic Ocean: Unexamined Risks, Unacceptable Consequences*, Commissioned by Pew Environment Group, November 2010.

[102] Government Accountability Office, *Coast Guard: Efforts to Identify Arctic Requirements Are Ongoing, but More Communication about Agency Planning Efforts Would Be Beneficial*, GAO-10-870, September 2010.

[103] Transportation Research Board of the National Academy of Sciences, *Risk of Vessel Accidents and Spills in the Aleutian Islands: Designing a Comprehensive Risk Assessment* (2008), Special Report 293, National Academies Press. Washington, DC.

[104] Coastal Response Research Center, *Opening the Arctic Seas: Envisioning Disasters and Framing Solutions*, (2009), partnership between the National Oceanic and Atmospheric Administration and the University of New Hampshire. See also, U.S. Arctic Research Commission, (Draft) *White Paper: U.S. Arctic Research Commission Recommends Steps to Expanded U.S. Funding for Arctic/Subarctic Oil Spill Research* (February 24, 2010).

[105] Arctic Monitoring and Assessment Programme (AMAP), *Arctic Oil and Gas 2007* (2008).

---

a slower rate in colder water temperatures. Although slower evaporation may allow for more oil to be recovered, evaporation removes the lighter, more toxic hydrocarbons that are present in crude oil.[106] The longer the oil remains in an ecosystem, the more opportunity there is for exposure. Oil spills may get trapped in ice, evaporating only when the ice thaws. In some cases, oil could remain in the ice for years.

Icy conditions enhance emulsification—the process of forming different states of water in oil, often described as "mousse." Emulsification creates oil cleanup challenges by increasing (1) the volume of the oil/water mixture and (2) the mixture's viscosity (resistance to flow). The latter change creates particular problems for conventional removal and pumping cleanup methods.[107] Moreover, two of the major non-mechanical recovery methods—in-situ burning and dispersant application—may be limited (or "precluded") by the Arctic conditions and lack of logistical support: aircraft, vessels, and other infrastructure.[108]

Existing Policy Framework

Considering both the recent increase in human activity in the region (and expectation of further interest) and the response and recovery challenges that an oil spill would impose in Arctic waters, many would assert that the region warrants particular attention in terms of governance. However, the existing framework for international governance of maritime operations in the Arctic region lacks legally binding requirements. While the Safety of Life at Sea Convention (SOLAS) and other International Maritime Organization (IMO) conventions include provisions regarding ships in icy waters, the provisions are not specific to the polar regions. The IMO has "Guidelines for Ships Operating in Arctic," but these were considered inadequate by many participants in a recent workshop.[109] As stated in a recent NOAA report, the non-binding IMO provisions seem "inconsistent with the hazards of Arctic navigation and the potential for environmental damage from such an incident."[110]

Fisheries[111]

Large commercial fisheries exist in the Arctic, including in the Barents and Norwegian Seas north of Europe, the Central North Atlantic off of Greenland and Iceland, and the Newfoundland and Labrador Seas off of northeastern Canada.[112]

---

[106] National Research Council, *Cumulative Environmental Effects of Oil and Gas Activities on Alaska's North Slope* (2003).

[107] Arturo A. Keller and Kristin Clark, *Oil Recovery with Novel Skimmer Surfaces under Cold Climate Conditions* (2007), prepared for the Minerals Management Service.

[108] World Wildlife Fund, *Oil Spill: Response Challenges in Arctic Waters* (2007). For further discussion of issues relating to oil spills, see CRS Report RL33705, *Oil Spills in U.S. Coastal Waters: Background and Governance*, by Jonathan L. Ramseur.

[109] Coastal Response Research Center, *Opening the Arctic Seas: Envisioning Disasters and Framing Solutions*, (2009), partnership between the National Oceanic and Atmospheric Administration and the University of New Hampshire.

[110] Coastal Response Research Center, *Opening the Arctic Seas: Envisioning Disasters and Framing Solutions*, (2009), partnership between the National Oceanic and Atmospheric Administration and the University of New Hampshire.

[111] This section prepared by Eugene Buck, Specialist in Natural Resources Policy, Resources, Science, and Industry Division.

[112] Erik J. Molenaar and Robert Corell, *Arctic Fisheries*, Arctic Transform, February 9, 2009; available at http://arctic-transform.org/download/FishBP.pdf.

In the 110th Congress, P.L. 110-243 stated that "the United States should initiate international discussions and take necessary steps with other Arctic nations to negotiate an agreement or agreements for managing migratory, transboundary, and straddling fish stocks in the Arctic Ocean and establishing a new international fisheries management organization or organizations for the region." In response to this, the United States participated in meetings with other Arctic nations at the March 2009 U.N. Food and Agriculture Organization Committee on Fisheries meetings in Rome. These international discussions are continuing.

On February 5, 2009, the North Pacific Fishery Management Council, acting under the authority of the Magnuson-Stevens Fishery Conservation and Management Act, unanimously approved the Council's draft Arctic Fisheries Management Plan and approved the preferred alternative, which would (1) close the Arctic to commercial fishing until information improves so that fishing can be conducted sustainably and with due concern to other ecosystem components; (2) determine the fishery management authorities in the Arctic and provide the Council with a vehicle for addressing future management issues; and (3) implement an ecosystem-based management policy that recognizes the resources of the U.S. Arctic and the potential for fishery development that might affect those resources, particularly in the face of a changing climate.

On November 3, 2009, the National Marine Fisheries Service (Department of Commerce) issued a final rule that implemented the North Pacific Council's Fishery Management Plan for Fish Resources of the Arctic Management Area, as well as Amendment 29 to the Fishery Management Plan for Bering Sea/Aleutian Islands King and Tanner Crabs. This action followed the North Pacific Council's recommendations establishing a basis for sustainable management of commercial fishing in the Arctic Management Area and moving the northern boundary of the crab fishery south of the Arctic Management Area to Bering Strait.[113]

Protected Species[114]

Concern over development of the Arctic relates to how such development might affect threatened and endangered species. Under the Endangered Species Act (16 U.S.C. §§1531-1543), the polar bear was listed as threatened on May 15, 2008. In addition, a positive 90-day finding was made on a petition to list the ribbon seal on March 28, 2008. The failure by the U.S. Fish and Wildlife Service to make a 90-day finding on a 2008 petition to list Pacific walrus has led to submission of 60-days' notice of a future citizen suit, and a petition to list ringed, bearded, and spotted seals was filed May 28, 2008.

In either terrestrial or marine environments, the extreme pace of change makes a biological response many times more difficult. For species with adaptations for a specific optimum temperature for egg development, or production of young timed to match the availability of a favored prey species, or seed dispersal in predictable fire regimes, etc., evolutionary responses may well not keep pace with the rate of change.[115] While species of plants and animals farther

---

[113] 74 *Federal Register* 56734-56746, November 3, 2009.

[114] Prepared by Lynne Corn and Eugene Buck, Specialists in Natural Resources Policy, Resources, Science, and Industry Division.

[115] Among biologists, it is traditionally said that a species faced with extreme change can respond in three basic ways: "migrate, mutate, or die." When change is rapid enough, mutation (accompanied by natural selection of individuals within the population more suited to the changed environment) may not be able to occur fast enough, leaving migration and death as the only options. The problem of response rate is more severe for species that reproduce slowly (e.g., polar (continued...)

---

south might migrate, drift, or be transplanted from warming habitats to more northerly sites that may continue to be suitable,[116] once a terrestrial species reaches the Arctic Ocean, it is very literally at the end of the line. No more northern or colder habitat is available.

The Marine Mammal Protection Act (MMPA; 16 U.S.C. §§1361 et seq.) protects whales, seals, walruses, and polar bears. The MMPA established a moratorium on the "taking" of marine mammals in U.S. waters and by U.S. nationals on the high seas, including the Arctic. The MMPA protects marine mammals from "clubbing, mutilation, poisoning, capture in nets, and other human actions that lead to extinction." Under the MMPA, the Secretary of Commerce, acting through National Marine Fisheries Service (NMFS), is responsible for the conservation and management of whales and seals. The Secretary of the Interior, acting through the Fish and Wildlife Service (FWS), is responsible for walruses and polar bears.[117] Despite the MMPA's general moratorium on taking, the MMPA allows U.S. citizens to apply for and obtain authorization for taking small numbers of mammals incidental to activities other than commercial fishing (e.g., offshore oil and gas exploration and development) if the taking would have only a negligible impact on any marine mammal species or stock, provided that monitoring requirements and other conditions are met.

Indigenous People Living in the Arctic[118]

Background

Seven of the eight Arctic nations have indigenous peoples,[119] whose predecessors were present in parts of the Arctic over 10,000 years ago, well before the arrival of peoples with European backgrounds.[120] Current Arctic indigenous peoples comprise dozens of diverse cultures and speak dozens of languages from eight or more non-Indo-European language families.[121]

Before the arrival of Europeans, Arctic indigenous peoples lived in economies that were chiefly dependent, in varying proportions, on hunting land and marine mammals, catching salt- and

---

(...continued)

bears) and less severe for species that reproduce rapidly (e.g., algae).

[116] The efficacy and the effect of this tactic is often questioned, since natural migration is unlikely to involve the entire suite of species in an ecosystem (e.g., host plants might not move north (or up) as fast as their moth herbivores, nor as fast as the birds that depend on the moths). Moreover, the southerners will not find a land of sterile bare dirt—the species that are already there may be threatened themselves by the competition from the new arrivals, perhaps tipping the balance and pushing still more species toward extinction.

[117] Under the MMPA, both NMFS and FWS have responsibility for additional marine mammal species (e.g., manatees, sea otters, dolphins) which are not currently found in the Arctic.

[118] This section prepared by Roger Walke, who was a Specialist in American Indian Policy, Domestic Social Policy Division, until his retirement from CRS in October 2010.

[119] *Arctic Human Development Report*, ed. Joan Nymand Larsen, et al. (Akureyri, Iceland: Stefansson Arctic Institute, 2004), p. 47; this report is subsequently cited in this section as *AHDR*. The seven countries are Canada, Denmark-Greenland, Finland, Norway, Russia, Sweden, and the United States.

[120] John F. Hoffecker, *A Prehistory of the North: Human Settlement of the Higher Latitudes* (New Brunswick, NJ: Rutgers University Press, 2005), pp. 8, 81, 112-115.

[121] *AHDR*, pp. 47, 53; David Crystal, *Cambridge Encyclopedia of Language*, 2nd ed. (Cambridge: Cambridge University Press, 1997), chap. 50; *Ethnologue: Languages of the World*, 16th ed., ed. M. Paul Lewis (Dallas: SIL International, 2009) available online at http://www.ethnologue.com/. The number of languages and language families varies not only with definitions of the Arctic but with definitions of languages and language families.

---

fresh-water fish, herding reindeer (in Eurasia), and gathering, for their food, clothing, and other products.[122] Indigenous peoples' interaction with and knowledge of Arctic wildlife and environments has developed over millennia and is the foundation of their cultures.[123]

The length of time that Arctic indigenous peoples were in contact with Europeans varied across the Arctic. As recorded by Europeans, contact began as early as the 9th century CE, if not before, in Fennoscandia[124] and northwestern Russia, chiefly for reasons of commerce (especially furs); it progressed mostly west-to-east across northern Asia, reaching northeastern Arctic Asia by the 17th century.[125] North American Arctic indigenous peoples' contact with Europeans started in Labrador in the 16th century and in Alaska in the 18th century, and was not completed until the early 20th century.[126] Greenland's indigenous peoples first saw European-origin peoples in the late 10th century, but those Europeans died out during the 15th or 16th century and Europeans did not return permanently until the 18th century.[127]

Contact led to significant changes in Arctic indigenous economies, political structures, foods, cultures, and populations, starting especially in the 20th century. At present, for instance, most Arctic indigenous peoples are minorities in their countries' Arctic areas, except in Greenland and Canada (one source estimates that, around 2003, about 10% of an estimated 3.7 million people in the Arctic were indigenous).[128] While many Arctic indigenous communities remain heavily dependent on hunting, fishing, and herding and are more likely to depend on traditional foods than non-indigenous Arctic inhabitants,[129] there is much variation. Most Arctic indigenous people may no longer consume traditional foods as their chief sources of energy and nutrition.[130] Major

---

[122] Jim Berner, et al., *Arctic Climate Impact Assessment* (Cambridge: Cambridge University Press, 2005), chapter 12; this report is subsequently cited in this section as *ACIA*.

[123] *ACIA*, pp. 654-655.

[124] Fennoscandia refers to the Scandinavian Peninsula, Finland, the Kola Peninsula of Russia, and certain parts of Russia bordering on Finland.

[125] Janet Martin, *Treasure in the Land of Darkness: The Fur Trade and Its Significance for Medieval Russia* (Cambridge: Cambridge University Press, 1986), pp. 41-42; James Forsyth, *A History of the Peoples of Siberia: Russia's North Asian Colony, 1581-1990* (Cambridge: Cambridge University Press, 1992), pp. 69-83, 102; Lassi K. Heininen, "Different Images of the Arctic and the Circumpolar North in World Politics," in *Knowledge and Power in the Arctic*, Proceedings at a Conference in Rovaniemi, April 16-18, 2007, Arctic Centre Reports 48, ed. Paula Kankaanpaa, et al. (Rovaniemi, Finland: University of Lapland, Arctic Centre, 2007), p. 125.

[126] James W. VanStone, "Exploration and Contact History of Western Alaska," and David Damas, "Copper Eskimo," and J. Garth Taylor, "Historical Ethnography of the Labrador Coast," in *Handbook of North American Indian: Vol. 5, Arctic*, vol. ed. David Damas, gen. ed. William C. Sturtevant (Washington: Smithsonian, 1984), pp. 149-155, 408, 509-510.

[127] Inge Kleivan, "History of Norse Greenland," in *Handbook, Vol. 5, Arctic, op. cit.*, pp. 549-555; Finn Gad, "Danish Greenland Policies," in *Handbook of North American Indians: Vol. 4, History of Indian-White Relations*, vol. ed. Wilcomb E. Washburn, gen. ed. William C. Sturtevant (Washington: Smithsonian, 1988), p. 110.

[128] *AHDR*, pp. 19, 29. Estimates of Arctic indigenous populations are complicated by varying definitions not only of the Arctic but also of indigenous peoples; for instance, Russia does not count some non-European Arctic ethnic groups, such as the Yakut, as "indigenous minorities" (see "Peoples of the Arctic: Characteristics of Human Populations Relevant to Pollution Issues," in *AMAP Assessment Report: Arctic Pollution Issues*, ed. Simon J. Wilson et al. (Oslo: Arctic Monitoring and Assessment Programme, 1998), pp. 167-169; this report is subsequently cited in this section as *AMAP 1998*.

[129] *AMAP 1998*, chapter 5; see also Birger Poppel et al., *SLiCA Results*, Survey of Living Conditions in the Arctic (Anchorage: Institute of Social and Economic Research, University of Alaska Anchorage, 2007), pp. 4-7, http://www.arcticlivingconditions.org.

[130] Annika E. Nilson and Henry P. Huntington, *Arctic Pollution 2009* (Oslo: Arctic Monitoring and Assessment Programme, 2009), p. 39-41; this report is subsequently cited in this section as *AMAP 2009*.

---

economic change is also relatively recent but ongoing.[131] Many Arctic indigenous communities have developed a mixture of traditional economic activities and wage employment.[132] Subsistence and economics will be key factors in the effects of climate change on Arctic indigenous peoples, and on their reaction to Arctic climate change.

Arctic indigenous peoples' current political structures vary, as do their relationships with their national governments. Some indigenous groups govern their own unique land areas within the national structure, as in the United States and Canada; others have special representative bodies, such as the Saami parliaments in Norway, Finland, and Sweden;[133] a few areas have general governments with indigenous majorities, such as Greenland (a member country of Denmark), Nunavut territory in Canada, and the North Slope and Northwest Arctic boroughs in Alaska.[134] Control of land, through claims and ownership, also varies among Arctic indigenous peoples, as do rights to fishing, hunting, and resources.[135] Arctic indigenous peoples' political relationships to their national and local governments, and their ownership or claims regarding land, are also significant factors in the responses to Arctic climate change by the indigenous peoples and by Arctic nations' governments.

Effects of Climate Change

Arctic climate change is expected to affect the economies, subsistence, health, population, societies, and cultures of Arctic indigenous peoples. Changes in sea ice and sea level, permafrost, tundra, and tree and vegetation distribution, and increased commercial shipping, will affect the distribution of land and sea mammals, of freshwater and marine fish, and of forage for reindeer, and this will in turn affect traditional subsistence activities and related indigenous lifestyles.[136] Arctic indigenous peoples' harvesting of animals is likely to become riskier and less predictable, which may increase food insecurity, change diets, and increase dependency on outside, non-traditional foods.[137] Sea and permafrost changes have damaged infrastructure and increased coastal erosion, especially in Alaska, where GAO found that "coastal villages are becoming more susceptible to flooding and erosion caused in part by rising temperatures."[138]

Oil, gas, and mineral exploration and development are expected to increase, as are other economic activities, such as forestry and tourism, and these are expected to increase economic opportunities for all Arctic residents, including indigenous peoples.[139] Pressures to increase participation in the wage economy, however, may speed up changes in indigenous cultures.

---

[131] *ACIA*, p. 1000.

[132] *SLiCA Results, op.cit.*, pp. v, 4-8.

[133] *AHDR*, p. 232.

[134] *AHDR*, chapter 4, and pp. 232-233.

[135] *AHDR*, chapters 6-7, and pp. 232-233.

[136] *ACIA*, pp. 1000-1001, 1004.

[137] *ACIA*, pp. 1000-1001, 1004.

[138] U.S. Government Accountability Office, *Alaska Native Villages: Villages Affected by Flooding and Erosion Have Difficulty Qualifying for Federal Assistance*, GAO-04-895T, June 29, 2004, p. i, http://www.gao.gov/new.items/ d04895t.pdf. See also, Government Accountability Office, *Alaska Native Villages: Most Are Affected by Flooding and Erosion, but Few Qualify for Federal Assistance*, GAO-04-142, December 12, 2003, http://www.gao.gov/new.items/ d04142.pdf.

[139] *ACIA*, pp. 1001, 1004.

Increased economic opportunities may also lead to a rise in the non-indigenous population, which may further change the circumstances of indigenous cultures.

Health problems may increase with Arctic climate change. Economic development may exacerbate Arctic pollution problems, including food contamination, and warmer temperatures may increase insect- and wildlife-borne diseases.[140] Climate change may lead to damage to water and sanitation systems, reducing protection against waterborne diseases.[141] Changes in Arctic indigenous cultures may increase mental stress and behavioral problems.[142]

The response to climate change by Arctic indigenous peoples has included international activities by Arctic indigenous organizations and advocacy before their national governments. As one report noted, "the rise of solidarity among indigenous peoples organizations in the region is surely a development to be reckoned with by all those interested in policy issues in the Arctic."[143] Six national or international indigenous organizations are permanent participants of the Arctic Council, the regional intergovernmental forum.[144] In April 2009, the Inuit Circumpolar Council (an organization of Inuit in the Arctic regions of Alaska, Canada, Greenland, and Russia) hosted in Alaska the worldwide "Indigenous Peoples Global Summit on Climate Change."[145] The conference report, forwarded to the Copenhagen Conference of the Parties of the U.N. Framework Convention on Climate Change (December 2009), noted "accelerating" climate change caused by "unsustainable development" and, among several recommendations, called for a greater indigenous role in national and international decisions on climate change, including a greater role for indigenous knowledge in climate change research, monitoring, and mitigation.[146] In Alaska, the Alaska Federation of Natives has asked Congress to mitigate flooding and erosion in Alaska Native villages and to fund relocation of villages where necessary.[147]

Polar Icebreaking[148]

The Coast Guard's polar icebreakers perform a variety of missions supporting U.S. interests in the Arctic (and Antarctic), including the following:

---

[140] *AMAP Assessment 2009: Human Health in the Arctic*, ed. Simon J. Wilson and Carolyn Symon (Oslo: Arctic Monitoring and Assessment Programme, 2009), pp. 4-6, 143.

[141] John Warren, "Climate change could affect human health," *Mukluk Telegraph*, January/February 2005, pp. 5-6.

[142] John Warren, "Climate change could affect human health," *Mukluk Telegraph*, January/February 2005, pp. 5-6.

[143] *AHDR*, p. 235.

[144] See http://www.arctic-council.org/. The six organizations are the Aleut International Association, Arctic Athabaskan Council, Gwich'in Council International, Inuit Circumpolar Council, RAIPON (Russian Association of Indigenous Peoples of the North), and Saami Council.

[145] See http://www.indigenoussummit.com/servlet/content/home.html.

[146] K. Galloway-McLean et al., *Report of the Indigenous Peoples' Global Summit on Climate Change: 20-24 April 2009, Anchorage, Alaska* (Darwin, Australia: United Nations University—Traditional Knowledge Initiative, 2009), pp. 5-7; available at http://www.indigenoussummit.com/servlet/content/home.html.

[147] Alaska Federation of Natives, Human Resources Committee, *2010 Federal Priorities* (Anchorage: Alaska Federation of Natives, 2010), pp. 22-23; available at http://www.nativefederation.org/documents/ 2010_AFN_Federal_Priorities.pdf. See also, Government Accountability Office, *Alaska Native Villages: Limited Progress Has Been Made on Relocating Villages Threatened by Flooding and Erosion*, GAO-09-551, June 3, 2009, http://www.gao.gov/new.items/d09551.pdf.

[148] This section prepared by Ronald O'Rourke, Specialist in Naval Affairs, Foreign Affairs, Defense, and Trade Division. It is adapted from CRS Report RL34391, *Coast Guard Polar Icebreaker Modernization: Background and Issues for Congress*, by Ronald O'Rourke.

- conducting and supporting U.S. scientific research in the Arctic;[149]

- defending U.S. sovereignty in the Arctic by helping to maintain a presence in the region;

- defending other U.S. interests in the Arctic, including economic interests relating to the U.S. exclusive economic zone (EEZ) north of Alaska;

- monitoring sea traffic in the Arctic, including ships bound for the United States; and

- conducting other typical Coast Guard missions (such as search and rescue, law enforcement, and protection of marine resources) in Arctic waters, including U.S. territorial waters north of Alaska.

The Coast Guard's proposed FY2013 budget includes $8 million in acquisition funding to initiate survey and design activities for a new polar icebreaker. The Coast Guard's Five Year Capital Investment Plan includes an additional $852 million in FY2014-FY2017 for acquiring the ship. The Coast Guard anticipates awarding a construction contract for the ship "within the next five years" and taking delivery on the ship "within a decade." The project to design and build a polar icebreaker is a new acquisition project initiated in the FY2013 budget.[150]

The Coast Guard's two existing heavy polar icebreakers—*Polar Star* and *Polar Sea*—have exceeded their intended 30-year service lives, and neither is currently operational. *Polar Star* was placed in caretaker status on July 1, 2006. Congress in FY2009 and FY2010 provided funding to repair it and return it to service for 7 to 10 years; the Coast Guard expects the reactivation project to be completed in December 2012. On June 25, 2010, the Coast Guard announced that *Polar Sea* had suffered an unexpected engine casualty; the ship was unavailable for operation after that. The Coast Guard placed *Polar Sea* in commissioned, inactive status on October 14, 2011, and plans to decommission it in FY2012.

The Coast Guard's third polar icebreaker—*Healy*—entered service in 2000. Compared to *Polar Star* and *Polar Sea*, *Healy* has less icebreaking capability (it is considered a medium polar icebreaker), but more capability for supporting scientific research. The ship is used primarily for supporting scientific research in the Arctic.

The reactivation of *Polar Star* and the decommissioning of *Polar Sea* will result in an operational U.S. polar icebreaking fleet consisting for the next 7 to 10 years of one heavy polar icebreaker (*Polar Star*) and one medium polar icebreaker (*Healy*). The new polar icebreaker for which initial acquisition funding is requested in the FY2013 budget would replace *Polar Star* at about the time *Polar Star's* 7- to 10-year reactivation period ends.

In July 2011, the Coast Guard provided to Congress a study on the Coast Guard's missions and capabilities for operations in high-latitude (i.e., polar) areas. The study, commonly known as the High Latitude Study and dated July 2010 on its cover, concluded the following:

---

[149] The Coast Guard's polar icebreakers also support U.S. scientific research in the Antarctic.

[150] Coast Guard FY2013-FY2017 Five Year Capital Investment Plan, as shown in U.S. Department of Homeland Security, *Annual Performance Report, Fiscal Years 2011 – 2013*, pp. CG-AC&I-12 and CG-AC&I-40 (pdf pages 1,749 and 1777 of 3,134).

- **The Coast Guard requires three heavy and three medium icebreakers to fulfill its statutory missions.** These icebreakers are necessary to (1) satisfy Arctic winter and transition season demands and (2) provide sufficient capacity to also execute summer missions. Single-crewed icebreakers have sufficient capacity for all current and expected statutory missions. Multiple crewing provides no advantage because the number of icebreakers required is driven by winter and shoulder season requirements. Future use of multiple or augmented crews could provide additional capacity needed to absorb mission growth.

- **The Coast Guard requires six heavy and four medium icebreakers to fulfill its statutory missions and maintain the continuous presence requirements of the Naval Operations Concept.** Consistent with current practice, these icebreakers are single-crewed and homeported in Seattle Washington.

- **Applying crewing and home porting alternatives reduces the overall requirement to four heavy and two medium icebreakers.** This assessment of non-material solutions shows that the reduced number of icebreakers can be achieved by having all vessels operate with multiple crews and two of the heavy icebreakers homeporting in the Southern Hemisphere.

Leasing was also considered as a nonmaterial solution. While there is no dispute that the Coast Guard's polar icebreaker fleet is in need of recapitalization, the decision to acquire this capability through purchase of new vessels, reconstruction of existing ships, or commercial lease of suitable vessels must be resolved to provide the best value to the taxpayer. The multi-mission nature of the Coast Guard may provide opportunities to conduct some subset of its missions with non government-owned vessels. However, serious consideration must be given to the fact that the inherently governmental missions of the Coast Guard must be performed using government-owned and operated vessels. An interpretation of the national policy is needed to determine the resource level that best supports the nation's interests....

The existing icebreaker capacity, two inoperative heavy icebreakers and an operational medium icebreaker, does not represent a viable capability to the federal government. The time needed to augment this capability is on the order of 10 years. At that point, around 2020, the heavy icebreaking capability bridging strategy expires.[151]

At a July 27, 2011, hearing on U.S. economic interests in the Arctic before the Oceans, Atmosphere, Fisheries, and Coast Guard subcommittee of the Senate Commerce, Science, and Transportation Committee, the following exchange occurred:

SENATOR OLYMPIA J. SNOWE: On the high latitude study, do you agree with—and those—I would like to also hear from you, Admiral Titley, as well, on these requirements in terms of Coast Guard vessels as I understand it, they want to have—I guess, it was a three medium ice breakers. Am in correct in saying that? Three medium ice breakers.

ADMIRAL ROBERT PAPP, COMMANDANT OF THE COAST GUARD: I agree with the mission analysis and as you look at the requirements for the things that we might do up there, if it is in the nation's interest, it identifies a minimum requirement for three heavy ice breakers and three medium ice breakers and then if you want a persistent presence up there, it would require—and also doing things such as breaking out (inaudible) and other responsibilities, then it would take up to a maximum six heavy and four medium.

---

[151] *United States Coast Guard High Latitude Region Mission Analysis Capstone Summary*, July 2010, pp. 12-13, 15.

SNOWE: Right. Do you agree with that?

PAPP: If we were to be charged with carrying out those full responsibilities, yes, ma'am. Those are the numbers that you would need to do it.

SNOWE: Admiral Titley, how would you respond to the high latitude study and has the Navy conducted its own assessment of its capability?

REAR ADMIRAL DAVID TITLEY, OCEANORGRAPHER AND NAVIGATOR OF THE NAVY: Ma'am, we are in the process right now of conducting what we call a capabilities based assessment that will be out in the summer of this year.

We are getting ready to finish that—the Coast Guard has been a key component of the Navy's task force on climate change, literally since day one when the Chief of Naval Operations set this up, that morning, we had the Coast Guard invited as a member of our executive steering committee.

So we have been working very closely with the Coast Guard, with the Department of Homeland Security, and I think Admiral Papp—said it best as far as the specific comments on the high latitude study but we have been working very closely with the Coast Guard.[152]

Potential issues for Congress regarding Coast Guard polar icebreaker modernization include the following:

- the potential impact on U.S. polar missions of the United States currently having no operational heavy polar icebreakers;

- the numbers and capabilities of polar icebreakers the Coast Guard will need in the future; the disposition of *Polar Sea* following its decommissioning;

- whether the new polar icebreaker initiated in the FY23013 budget should be funded with incremental funding (as proposed in the Coast Guard's Five Year Capital Investment Plan) or full funding in a single year, as required under the executive branch's full funding policy;

- whether new polar icebreakers should be funded entirely in the Coast Guard budget, or partly or entirely in some other part of the federal budget, such as the Department of Defense (DOD) budget, the National Science Foundation (NSF) budget, or both;

- whether to provide future icebreaking capability through construction of new ships or service life extensions of existing polar icebreakers; and whether future polar icebreakers should be acquired through a traditional acquisition or a leasing arrangement.

---

[152] Source: Transcript of hearing.

Search and Rescue[153]

General

The possibility of increased sea and air traffic through Arctic waters has increased concerns regarding Arctic-area search and rescue capabilities. Given the location of current U.S. Coast Guard operating bases, it could take Coast Guard aircraft several hours, and Coast Guard cutters days or even weeks, to reach a ship or a downed aircraft in distress in Arctic waters. In addition, the harsh climate complicates search and rescue operations in the region. Particular concern has been expressed about cruise ships that may experience problems and need assistance; there have already been incidents of this kind in recent years in waters off Antarctica. A May 7, 2011, press report stated:

> U.S. and Canadian military commanders say they are examining their rescue capabilities in the Arctic as a shrinking ice cap brought about by climate change opens up rich oil and gas reserves and draws more commercial traffic to the top of the globe....
>
> [U.S. Admiral James Winnefeld, commander of the U.S. Northern Command and the North American Aerospace Defense Command, or NORAD] and NORAD'S deputy commander, Canadian Forces Lt. Gen. Marcel Duval, said more ships in the Arctic Ocean - and more jetliners crossing Arctic skies - could mean more emergencies.
>
> "More ships, more chances of accidents," Duval said in a separate interview in his office at NORAD headquarters at Peterson.
>
> Last summer, the Canadian Coast Guard rescued 197 people from the cruise ship Clipper Adventurer, which ran aground inside the Arctic Circle....
>
> Sea traffic is still light, with only about 25 ships a year currently crossing the maritime Arctic boundary between Alaska and the Yukon. But that number is increasing by 10 to 15 percent a year, according to NORAD statistics.
>
> Civilian air traffic over the Arctic is booming. U.S. and Canadian aviation agencies report more than 9,600 civilian flights across the North Pole in 2010, up nearly 21 percent from 2008.[154]

One option for mitigating the risks associated with cruise ship operations in the Arctic would be to require the vessels to sail in pairs, so that if one ship experiences a problem, the other one could quickly come to its aid.

Increasing U.S. Coast Guard search and rescue capabilities for the Arctic could require one or more of the following: enhancing or creating new Coast Guard operating bases in the region; procuring additional Arctic-capable aircraft, cutters, and rescue boats for the Coast Guard; and adding systems to improve Arctic maritime communications, navigation, and domain

---

[153] This section prepared by Ronald O'Rourke, Specialist in Naval Affairs, Foreign Affairs, Defense, and Trade Division.

[154] Dan Elliott, "NORAD Chiefs Eye Busier Arctic," *Fairbanks Daily News-Miner*, May 7, 2011.

awareness.[155] It may also entail enhanced forms of cooperation with navies and coast guards of other Arctic countries.

Coast Guard Statements

A January 2011 press report summarized remarks made by the Commandant of the Coast Guard, Admiral Robert Papp, concerning Coast Guard search and rescue capabilities in the Arctic. The article quoted Papp as saying that there is a need for a range of Coast Guard operational capability for the Arctic, and that "In the meantime, he said the service will lean on partnerships with other Arctic nations. However, he warned that the Coast Guard will likely not be able to respond to any crises in the Arctic circle in a timely fashion. He recalled that the Canadian Coast Guard came under fire when it took six days to rescue a cruise ship and oil tanker that both ran aground in its northern waters." The article stated:

> "We wouldn't be able to make it in six days," he said. "It'd probably take us six weeks to get adequate resources up for a similar thing in our waters, so we have to start focusing on this."[156]

A March 2011 press report summarizing remarks made by Admiral Papp during and after a hearing before the Coast Guard and Maritime Transportation subcommittee of the House Transportation and Infrastructure Committee stated:

> Because retreating ice continues to make the passageways in the Arctic Ocean more navigable, the Coast Guard needs to have air stations in the region to conduct helicopter rescue missions, Papp said. He has not chosen specific cities for the air station sites, but he said the Alaskan cities of Barrow and Kotzebue come to mind.

> When lawmakers focus on Arctic resources, the United States' shortage of icebreakers usually draws the bulk of attention, but Papp said the Coast Guard is also in dire need of small boats to conduct rescue missions.[157]

At a June 23, 2011, hearing on the Coast Guard's proposed FY2012 budget before the Oceans, Atmosphere, Fisheries, and Coast Guard subcommittee of the Senate Commerce, Science, and Transportation Committee, the following exchange occurred:

> ADMIRAL ROBERT J. PAPP, JR., COMMANDANT OF THE COAST GUARD: I visited Barrow, Kotzebue, and Nome. And, actually, it was a revisit because I had served up there as an ensign (ph) 35 years ago. And so it was good to get back up there and see the changes.

> But what has not changed is the infrastructure up there. And I think that we have to have a robust discussion on the infrastructure needed to support what is no doubt going to be an increase in human activity up there off the – the North Coast of Alaska.

---

[155] For a report assessing certain emergency scenarios in the Arctic, including search and rescue scenarios, see *Opening the Arctic Seas, Envisioning Disasters and Framing Solutions*, Coastal Response and Research Center, University of New Hampshire, report of January 2009, based on conference held March 18-20, 2008, at Durham, New Hampshire.

[156] Cid Standifer, "Coast Guard Comandant: Service Still Committed To Eight NSCs," Inside the Navy, January 17, 2011.

[157] Jennifer Scholtes, "Papp: Coast Guard Arctic Plan Must Look Beyond Icebreakers," *CQ Homeland Security*, March 1, 2011.

Icebreakers I think are important, but they cloud the discussion of the other needs that we have up there. And I think we've focused on icebreakers over the last few years, even though they are important...

SENATOR MARK BEGICH: Right.

PAPP: ... and needed. But, right now, if we were to have to mount a response like we did in the Gulf of Mexico—I sent 3,000 people down for Deepwater Horizon. You know how many hotel rooms are available in Barrow.

BEGICH: That's right.

PAPP: And we—we have no place to put people up there. We have no hangars for aircraft. We have no piers, no Coast Guard boats. So my immediate, pressing concern is as human activity occurs, as you have that ship that goes through that—first of all, we'll assure safety standards because no matter where ships operate in the world, we are involved in their safety standards.

But if an accident happens, how do we respond? And, right now, we've got zero capability to respond in the Arctic right now. And we've got to do better than that.

That—when people ask me what keeps me awake at night—an oil spill, a collision, a ship sinking in the Arctic keeps me awake at night because we have nothing to respond or, if we respond, it's going to take us weeks to get there.[158]

State Department Statement

The State Department states that:

the United States and the seven other Arctic Council (AC) Member States (Canada, Denmark, Finland, Iceland, Norway, Russian Federation, Sweden) adopted a Ministerial Declaration in April 2009 in Tromso, Norway, which established a Task Force with the mandate of developing a Search and Rescue (SAR) agreement for the Arctic. The United States hosted the first meeting of the Arctic SAR Task Force during December 9-11, 2009, in Washington, D.C. The next round of negotiations is scheduled [sic] for February 25-26, 2010, in Moscow, Russian Federation. The Arctic SAR Task Force has been asked to finalize the Arctic SAR agreement such that it can be presented for adoption by the AC at its Ministerial meeting in Spring 2011.

The United States is at the forefront of efforts to promote safety in the Arctic. The Department of State's Office of Ocean and Polar Affairs is coordinating federal interagency interest to negotiate an instrument for the saving of lives at sea and the rescue of survivors after aircraft accidents in the Arctic. The U.S. Coast Guard is a prominent agency participating in this effort. With so few resources available for SAR in the Arctic, developing a regional agreement to set baseline standards for greater international cooperation and coordination will be of great value.[159]

---

[158] Source: Transcript of hearing.

[159] Source: State Department website accessed at http://www.state.gov/g/oes/ocns/opa/arc/c29382.htm on July 7, 2011.

Arctic Council Agreement on Arctic Search and Rescue (May 2011)

On May 12, 2011, representatives from the member states of the Arctic Council, meeting in Nuuk, Greenland, signed an agreement on cooperation on aeronautical and maritime search and rescue in the Arctic. Secretary of State Hillary Rodham Clinton signed for the United States. Key features of the agreement include the following:

- Article 2 states: "The objective of this Agreement is to strengthen aeronautical and maritime search and rescue cooperation and coordination in the Arctic."

- Article 3 and the associated Annex to the agreement essentially divide the Arctic into search and rescue areas within which each party has primary responsibility for conducting search and rescue operations, stating that "the delimitation of search and rescue regions is not related to and shall not prejudice the delimitation of any boundary between States or their sovereignty, sovereign rights or jurisdiction," and that "each Party shall promote the establishment, operation and maintenance of an adequate and effective search and rescue capability within its area."

- Article 4 and the associated Appendix I to the agreement identify the competent authority for each party. For the United States, the competent authority is the Coast Guard.

- Article 5 and the associated Appendix II to the agreement identify the agencies responsible for aeronautical and maritime search and rescue for each party. For the United States, those agencies are the Coast Guard and the Department of Defense.

- Article 6 and the associated Appendix III to the agreement identify the aeronautical and/or maritime rescue coordination centers (RCCs) for each party. For the United States, the RCCs are Joint Rescue Coordination Center Juneau (JRCC Juneau) and Aviation Rescue Coordination Center Elmendorf (ARCC Elmendorf).

- Article 7 states that "the Parties shall conduct aeronautical and maritime search and rescue operations pursuant to this Agreement consistent" with certain general guidelines.[160]

---

[160] The guidelines, as stated in Article 7, are as follows:

(a) search and rescue operations conducted pursuant to this Agreement in the territory of a Party shall be carried out consistent with the laws and regulations of that Party;

(b) if a search and rescue agency and/or RCC of a Party receives information that any person is, or appears to be, in distress, that Party shall take urgent steps to ensure that the necessary assistance is provided;

(c) any Party having reason to believe that a person, a vessel or other craft or aircraft is in a state of emergency in the area of another Party as set forth in paragraph 2 of the Annex shall forward as soon as possible all available information to the Party or Parties concerned;

(d) the search and rescue agency and/or RCC of a Party that has received information concerning a situation provided for in subparagraph (b) of this paragraph may request assistance from the other Parties;

(e) the Party to whom a request for assistance is submitted shall promptly decide on and inform the
(continued...)

- Article 8 states that "a Party requesting permission to enter the territory of a Party or Parties for search and rescue purposes, including for refueling, shall send its request to a search and rescue agency and/or RCC of the relevant Party or Parties," and that "the Party receiving such a request shall immediately confirm such receipt. The receiving Party, through its RCCs, shall advise as soon as possible as to whether entry into its territory has been permitted and the conditions, if any, under which the mission may be undertaken."

- Article 9 states that "the Parties shall enhance cooperation among themselves in matters relevant to this Agreement," that "the Parties shall exchange information that may serve to improve the effectiveness of search and rescue operations," and that "the Parties shall promote mutual search and rescue cooperation by giving due consideration to collaborative efforts."

- Article 10 states that "the Parties shall meet on a regular basis in order to consider and resolve issues regarding practical cooperation."

- Article 11 states that "after a major joint search and rescue operation, the search and rescue agencies of the Parties may conduct a joint review of the operation led by the Party that coordinated the operation."

- Article 12 states that "unless otherwise agreed, each Party shall bear its own costs deriving from its implementation of this Agreement," and that "implementation of this Agreement shall be subject to the availability of relevant resources."

- Article 18 states that "any Party to this Agreement may, where appropriate, seek cooperation with States not party to this Agreement that may be able to contribute to the conduct of search and rescue operations, consistent with existing international agreements."

- Article 19 states that "any Party may at any time withdraw from this Agreement by sending written notification thereof to the depositary[161] through diplomatic channels at least six months in advance."[162]

Figure 4 shows an illustrative map of the national areas of search and rescue responsibility based on the geographic coordinates listed in the Annex to the agreement.

(...continued)

requesting Party whether or not it is in a position to render the assistance requested and shall promptly indicate the scope and the terms of the assistance that can be rendered;

(f) the Parties shall ensure that assistance be provided to any person in distress. They shall do so regardless of the nationality or status of such a person or the circumstances in which that person is found; and

(g) a Party shall promptly provide all relevant information regarding the search and rescue of any person to the consular or diplomatic authorities concerned.

[161] Article 20 identifies the government of Canada as the depository for the agreement.

[162] Source: Text of final version of agreement made ready for signing and dated April 21, 2011, accessed July 7, 2011, at http://arctic-council.org/filearchive/Arctic_SAR_Agreement_EN_FINAL_for_signature_21-Apr-2011.pdf

Figure 4. Illustrative Map of Arctic SAR Areas in Arctic SAR Agreement

(Based on geographic coordinates listed in the agreement)

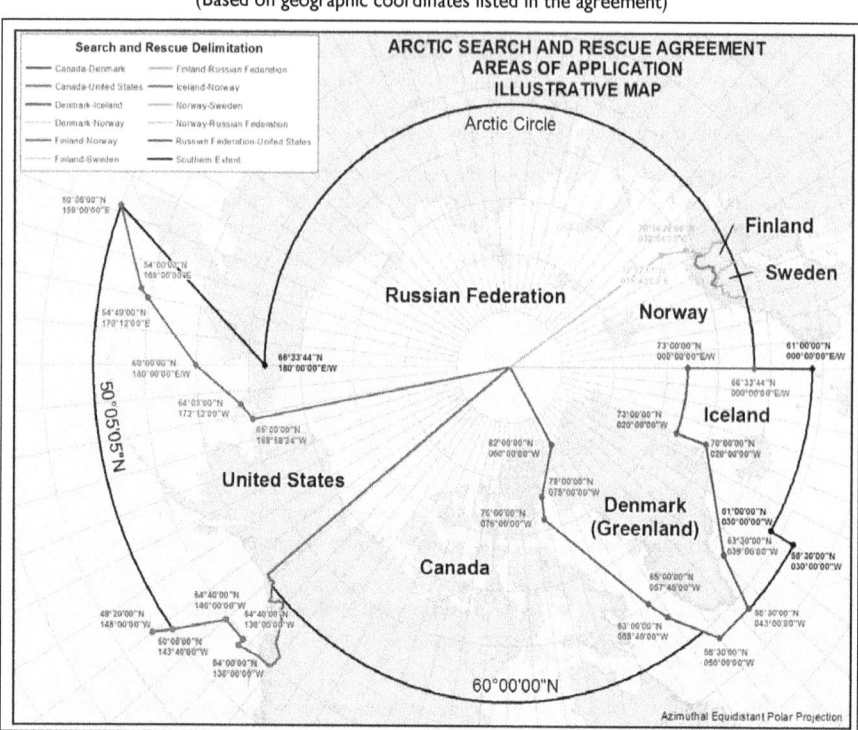

Source: "Arctic Search and Rescue Agreement," accessed July 7, 2011 at http://www.arcticportal.org/features/features-of-2011/arctic-search-and-rescue-agreement.

The State Department states that the agreement:

> is the first legally-binding instrument negotiated under the auspices of the Arctic Council. It coordinates life-saving international maritime and aeronautical SAR coverage and response among the Arctic States across an area of about 13 million square miles in the Arctic.

> As Arctic sea ice coverage decreases, ship-borne activities are increasing significantly in the Arctic. Flight traffic is also on the rise as new polar aviation routes cross the Arctic air space in several directions. As human presence and activities in the Arctic expand, the potential for accidents increases as well. Limited rescue resources, challenging weather conditions, and the remoteness of the area render SAR operations difficult in the Arctic, making coordination among the Arctic nations imperative. The SAR Agreement will improve search and rescue response in the Arctic by committing all Parties to coordinate appropriate assistance to those in distress and to cooperate with each other in undertaking SAR operations. For each Party, the Agreement defines an area of the Arctic in which it will have lead responsibility in organizing responses to SAR incidents, both large and small. Parties to the Agreement commit to provide SAR assistance regardless of the nationality or status of persons who may need it.

The Arctic Council launched this initiative at its 2009 Ministerial Meeting in Tromso, Norway, establishing a Task Force, co-chaired by the United States and the Russian Federation. The Task Force proceeded in a highly collaborative spirit, meeting five times (in Washington, Moscow, Oslo, Helsinki and Reykjavik).

The signature of the SAR Agreement in Nuuk is a positive step toward building partnerships in the Arctic. In particular, it reflects the commitment of the Arctic Council States to enhance their cooperation and offer responsible assistance to those involved in accidents in one of the harshest environments on Earth.

This Agreement illustrates one of the most successful negotiations to date to address emerging issues in the Arctic. Arctic Council participants approached SAR negotiations with collaboration and dedication to a positive outcome. The United States congratulates its colleagues in this effort and looks forward to further collaboration on the vital issues facing the rich but fragile Arctic region.[163]

Geopolitical Environment[164]

Many observers have noted that the loss of Arctic ice[165] is already leading to stepped-up human activity in the high north, particularly in the form of increasing commercial traffic and development. This trend has brought forth a range of issues on the geopolitical front, from environmental protection to search-and-rescue capabilities to the delineation of national boundaries—which will determine access to natural resources. These concerns are being addressed cooperatively in both bilateral and multilateral fashion, especially under the aegis of the Arctic Council and the U.N. Convention on the Law of the Sea (UNCLOS). Nonetheless, some observers continue to raise questions concerning security in the high north, and have advanced sometimes conflicting views regarding the potential roles of military forces in the region. Of the other Arctic coastal nations, the United States enjoys strong political and commercial ties with Canada, Norway, and Denmark; all four countries are members of NATO. Although the United States views Russia as an important partner in developing policies to cope with changing conditions in the Arctic, relations with Moscow have been somewhat problematic. Several non-Arctic nations, including India and China, have also evinced interest in gaining permanent observer status in the Arctic Council. In addition, the European Union, which sought but was denied full observer status in 2009, is nonetheless developing policy toward the Arctic.[166]

Multilateral Cooperation

As noted elsewhere in this report (see "Territorial Claims and Sovereignty Issues"), in late May 2008, ministerial representatives of the five Arctic littoral states attended a meeting convened by Denmark in Ilulissat, Greenland (a semi-autonomous territory of Denmark). Danish Foreign

---

[163] Source: State Department website accessed at http://www.state.gov/r/pa/prs/ps/2011/05/163285.htm on July 7, 2011.

[164] This section prepared by Carl Ek, Specialist in International Relations, Foreign Affairs, Defense, and Trade Division.

[165] "Arctic Sea Ice Continues to Decline, Hits Near Record Low," *IB Times*, October 4, 2011.

[166] "China, India Enter Heating-up Arctic Race," *Asia Times*, January 25, 2012. "Aston in Far North to Reach EU Policy on Arctic," *Agence France Presse*, March 8, 2012. "EU Application to Arctic Council Postponed," North Norway European Office, May 18, 2011 http://www.northnorway.org/nyheter/847-eu-application-to-arctic-council-postponed See also: "Arctic Governance: Balancing Challenges and Development," European Parliament Regional Briefing 2012, DG EXPO/B/PolDep/Note/2012_136 June, 2012

Minister Stig Møller implied that the meeting was intended to develop interim measures for Arctic governance: "We must continue to fulfill our obligations in the Arctic area until the U.N. decides who will have the right to the sea and the resources in the region. We must agree on the rules and what to do if climate changes make more shipping possible."[167] Attendees discussed a variety of issues, including the environment, transportation, resources, and security. The Danish Foreign Ministry stated that the resulting Ilulissat Declaration

> sent a clear political signal to the local inhabitants and the rest of the world that we will act responsibly when addressing the development in the Arctic Ocean. We have committed ourselves politically to solve any disagreements through negotiation. Thus, hopefully, we have eradicated all the myths about a 'race for the North Pole.' The legal framework is in place and the five States have now declared that they will abide by it.[168]

The Arctic has increasingly become a subject of discussions in bilateral meetings among leaders of the nations in the region. The main international forum for cooperation in the high north, however, is the eight-nation Arctic Council, of which the United States is an active member. The chief topics addressed by the six working groups of the Council, which was formed in 1996, are sustainable development, environmental protection, and the social well-being of the indigenous communities. The United States vetoed security as an issue of consideration for the Council. The Council holds ministerial-level meetings biennially, while the working groups meet more frequently. Sweden currently holds the two-year revolving Council chairmanship; Canada will take over in 2013, followed by the United States.[169]

On May 11-12, 2011, Secretary of State Hillary Clinton attended the most recent Arctic Council ministerial summit, held in Nuuk, Greenland; she was accompanied by U.S. Interior Secretary Ken Salazar. They were the first U.S. Cabinet members to attend an Arctic Council meeting, and observers noted that their visits served to raise the profile of Arctic issues. The meeting was led by Sweden, which currently chairs the Council. Noting the increased commercial activity in the region, Secretary Clinton stated, "We need to pursue these opportunities in a smart, sustainable way that preserves the Arctic environment and ecosystem."[170] Among other issues, attendees focused on efforts to reduce emissions that cause "black carbon" to settle on the Arctic region, accelerating ice melt. In addition, the Council discussed launching a longer-term study on methods to cope with possible future oil spills.

The major "deliverable" of the summit, however, was the signing of an Agreement on Cooperation on Aeronautical and Maritime Search and Rescue (SAR) in the Arctic. The accord was hailed as the "first legally-binding instrument negotiated under the auspices of the Arctic Council." The SAR initiative, developed mainly by the United States and Russia, had been

---

[167] Conference on the Arctic Ocean, May 26, 2008, Arctic Council website: http://arctic-council.org/article/2008/5/conference_on_the_arctic_ocean.

[168] Conference In Ilulissat, Greenland: Landmark Political Declaration on the Future of the Arctic, Edited December 11, 2008, website of the Danish Foreign Ministry, http://www.um.dk/en.

[169] The Council members are the "Arctic 5" coastal States plus Sweden, Finland, and Iceland. Six indigenous Arctic peoples organizations are permanent participants. Several other countries, including Spain, China, and the UK, have observer status. For additional information, see the Arctic Council's website: http://www.arctic-council.org/index.php/en/. "Document On Cooperation In Arctic Search and Rescue Efforts Could Be Ready In April 2011," *Interfax: Russia & CIS Military Newswire*, February 26, 2010.

[170] "States Set Rules on Exploiting Arctic Wealth," *Agence France Presse*, May 12, 2011.

---

introduced during the April 2009 summit. The Council also approved the establishment of a permanent secretariat, to be based in Tromsø, Norway.[171]

In early June 2012, Secretary Clinton traveled once more to the Arctic, visiting the new secretariat in Tromsø as part of an eight-day trip to Scandinavia. While there, she emphasized that the United States "want[s] the Arctic Council to remain the premier institution that deals with Arctic questions."[172]

Analysts note that Russia is keen to capitalize on natural resource development and shipping in the Arctic. As noted elsewhere in this report, Russia and Norway in late 2010 resolved a 40-year dispute over national borders in the Barents Sea; the accord will permit exploration for undersea oil, believed to be in rich supply there. In addition, scientists estimate that the sea route along the Siberian coast (referred to as the Northeast Passage or the Northern Sea Route, or NSR) will be ice-free and navigable well before the Northwest Passage through the Canadian archipelago; 34 vessels sailed the NSR in 2011. Russia sees significant economic opportunities in offering icebreaker escorts, refueling posts, and supplies to the commercial ships that will use the waterway.[173] But Russian leaders also understand that doing so will require international cooperation and goodwill. In August 2012, Russia is scheduled to join the United States and Norway in the military exercise *Northern Eagle 2012.*[174]

Although its borders lie some distance from the Arctic, China has also displayed a growing interest in the region, based mainly upon the potential opportunities for shorter sea routes and the eventual development of energy-related natural resources. China's economy is strongly dependent upon exports; some analysts have estimated that as much as one-half of China's GDP is reliant upon exports and shipping. China also is reliant upon ocean transportation for its large petroleum imports. The opening of Arctic sea corridors north of Russia and/or Canada would drastically reduce both sailing times and transportation costs. Beijing is keenly interested in having free access to these future waterways.

Many Chinese believe that the Arctic should be considered as part of the global commons. According to David Curtis Wright of the Naval War College, "The mantra that the Arctic and its natural resource wealth belong to no one country but constitute the common heritage of all humankind is virtually de rigueur in recent Chinese public commentary on Arctic affairs."[175] During a May 2012 workshop on Sino-Nordic cooperation hosted in Beijing, Chinese participants referred to their country as a "near-Arctic state" and a "stakeholder." Some analysts believe that

---

[171] "Secretary Clinton Signs the Arctic Search and Rescue Agreement with Other Arctic Nations," U.S. Department of State website, May 12, 2011. "Warming Arctic Opens Way to Competition For Resources," *Washington Post*, May 16, 2011.

[172] "Clinton in Arctic to See Impact of Climate Change," *Agence France Presse*, June 2, 2012.

[173] During an October 2011 conference on Arctic shipping, President Putin enthused that "the Arctic is the shortcut between the largest markets of Europe and the Asia-Pacific region.... It is an excellent opportunity to optimize costs." "Warming Revives Dream of Sea Route in Russian Arctic," *New York Times*, October 17, 2011.

[174] "Foreign Ministers of Russia and Canada Agreed To Go To the Ice Without the Third Parties," *WPS: Defense & Security*, September 20, 2010. "Russia Will Staunchly Defend its Interests in the Arctic Region – Putin," *Interfax*, June 30, 2011. "Russia to Deploy Troops to Defend Interests in Arctic," *Wall Street Journal*, July 2, 2011. "Russia, U.S., Norway to Hold Joint Naval Drills in August," *RIA Novosti*, May 24, 2012 http://en.rian.ru/world/20120524/173654802.html.

[175] "The Dragon Eyes the Top of the World," David Curtis Wright, Naval War College, China Maritime Studies Institute, Number 8, August 2011.

China will likely remain officially circumspect on this question, as its "foreign policy rests a profound respect for territorial integrity...."[176] Nonetheless, some Chinese analysts reportedly are encouraging the government to challenge Canada's claim of sovereignty over the Northwest Passage. China has also been active in conducting research on the Arctic; it acquired a large icebreaker in 1993 and has constructed a state-of-the-art polar capable research vessel, the *Snow Dragon*. In April 2012, Chinese Premier Wen Jiabao visited Sweden and Iceland, and two months later President Hu Jintao went to Denmark; the two leaders were reportedly discussing large-scale investments in the region. In addition, China (like several other nations) has established a research station in the Svalbard archipelago and has beefed up the size of its embassy staff in Iceland.

Security Issues

Throughout the Cold War, the Arctic region was a zone of strategic interest, where the United States, the Soviet Union, and allied states conducted air and naval maneuvers and tested ballistic missiles. With the collapse of the Warsaw Pact and the Soviet Union, however, the importance of the high north diminished in the 1990s. Although the establishment of sovereignty through the demarcation of boundaries in the region is being conducted peacefully under the auspices of the U.N. Convention on the Law of the Sea (UNCLOS), the Arctic is once again being viewed by some as a potential emerging security issue. In a December 2011 *Washington Post* op-ed, Heather Conley, a senior fellow at the Center for Strategic and International Studies, noted several recent developments:

> In April [2011], President Obama signed a new command plan that gives NORAD and the U.S. Northern Command greater responsibility in protecting the North Pole and U.S. Arctic territory. ... In 2009, Norway moved its operational command to its northern territories above the Arctic Circle. Russia has plans to establish a brigade that is specially equipped and prepared for military warfare in Arctic conditions. Denmark has made it a strategic priority to form an Arctic Command. Canada is set to revitalize its Arctic fleet, including spending $33 billion to build 28 vessels over the next 30 years.[177]

Canadian academic Rob Huebert has pointed out that in August 2010 the United States, Canada, and Denmark conducted in the Canadian Arctic their annual joint naval exercises involving several advanced and powerful warships. Huebert observed that "while defence officials are quick to point out they see no military threat to the region, it's still interesting to see these three Arctic friends coming together to improve their naval combat capability in the Far North."[178] In varying degrees, the Arctic coastal states have indicated a willingness to establish and maintain a military presence in the high north.[179] Although some have argued that terrorism and hijacking may constitute security concerns in the region, others maintain that such threats are chimerical, given

---

[176] "China Defines Itself as a 'Near-Arctic State,' Says SIPRI," Swedish International Peace Research Institute, May 10, 2012. "China's Arctic Ambitions," *Stratfor*, June 18, 2012. "China: Icebreaking in the Arctic," *The ISN Blog*, May 4, 2012. "Ice Station Dragon: China's Strategic Arctic Interest," *Defense News*, May 16, 2011.

[177] Heather Conley, "The Colder War: U.S., Russia and Others Are Vying for Control of Santa's Back Yard," *Washington Post*, December 23, 2011.

[178] "Welcome To a New Era of Arctic Security," Rob Huebert, Canadian Defense and Foreign Affairs Institute, August, 2010.

[179] See, for example, "Canada Vows 'Firm' Defence of Arctic Border," *Canwest News Service*, November 24, 2009. "Danes With Dogs To Join Military Sovereignty Patrol Of Canadian Arctic," *The Canadian Press*, March 3, 2010. "Norway Plans One New Arctic Base, Perhaps More," *Defense News*, March 8, 2010.

---

the challenges of distance and geography, and the difficulty of navigating in a polar environment. *The Economist* has asserted that "… the risks of Arctic conflict have been exaggerated. Most of the Arctic is clearly assigned to individual countries. According to a Danish estimate, 95% of Arctic mineral resources are within agreed national boundaries."[180]

The Arctic has also become a region of interest for NATO. However, as one writer has noted, "[t]here is currently no consensus within the alliance that NATO has any role to play in the Arctic, as Canada strongly opposes any NATO involvement on sovereignty grounds and other NATO members are concerned with negative Russian reaction."[181] Speaking in Reykjavík in January 2009, former NATO Secretary General Jaap de Hoop Scheffer urged that member states not allow the Arctic to become a divisive issue. He also recommended that the alliance and Russia cooperate through building upon their shared experience in search-and-rescue operations. Former Danish Prime Minister Anders Fogh Rasmussen, who became secretary general of the alliance in August 2009, has also addressed security in the high north. Citing the "potentially huge security implications" of Arctic climate change, Rasmussen in October 2009 stated that "I think it is within the natural scope of work for NATO to be the forum for consultation and discussion on [selected Arctic] issues."[182] In March 2009, however, Russia's NATO ambassador stated that Moscow would not cooperate with the alliance on Arctic matters. And in September 2010, President Medvedev reportedly observed that "the Arctic can do fine without NATO," and that his government "views [possible NATO] activity with quite serious tension, because it is after all a zone of peaceful cooperation, economic cooperation, and of course the military factor always—at a minimum—creates additional questions." On a visit to Moscow in November 2010, Rasmussen assured the Russians that NATO does not intend to establish a presence in the Arctic.[183] Since 2006, several member and partner states have participated in *Cold Response*, a wide-ranging annual crisis response exercise hosted by Norway. During the most recent joint maneuvers in March 2012, 14 nations fielded air, land, and naval assets and more than 16,000 troops. Although the exercises are multilateral, they are not conducted under the auspices of NATO.[184]

It has been noted that Russia "has at least half of the Arctic in terms of area, coastline, population and probably mineral wealth…."[185] The Russian government has stated that, although it deplores the notion of an arms race in the region and does not foresee a conflict there, it intends to protect

---

[180] "The Arctic: Special Report," *The Economist*, June 16, 2012. p. 10.

[181] "A New Security Architecture for the Arctic: An American Perspective," Center for Strategic and International Studies (CSIS), January 2012, p. 30.

[182] Nonetheless, one analyst has noted that the word "Arctic" does not appear either in the 2010 NATO Strategic Concept, nor in the Summit Declaration of the 2012 Chicago Summit – likely at the insistence of Canada. See "NATO in the Arctic: Challenges and Opportunities," by Luke Coffee, Heritage Foundation Issue Brief No. 3646, June 22, 2012.

[183] "Russia, Norway Sign Border Deal For Arctic Energy," *Reuters*, September 15, 2010. "NATO Chief Cautions Against Division Over Arctic," *Canwest News Service*, January 29, 2009. "NATO Proposes Arctic Cooperation With Russia," Reuters, January 29, 2009. Speech by NATO Secretary General Jaap de Hoop Scheffer On Security Prospects In the High North, January 29, 2009, http://www.nato.int/docu/speech/2009/s090129a.html. "NATO Chief Wars Of Climate Change Security Risks," *Agence France Presse*, October 1, 2009. "Rogozin Says He Won't Discuss Cooperation In Arctic With NATO," *Interfax: Russia & CIS General Newswire*, March 27, 2009.

[184] "NATO Tests Its Forces in Arctic," February 16, 2012, Atlantic Council web page: http://www. acus.org/natosource/nato-tests-its-forces-arctic "NATO, Russia Stage Arctic War Games," April 25, 2012 Atlantic Council web page: http://www. acus.org/print/68922 See also Cold Response 2012, Norwegian Armed Forces web page: http://mil.no/excercises/coldresponse2012/pages/default.aspx

[185] "The Arctic: Special Report," *The Economist*, June 16, 2012. p. 11.

---

its Arctic interests.[186] However, Russia has at times appeared to be sending out mixed messages. For example, at the conclusion of a meeting in September 2010, Russian Foreign Minister Sergei Lavrov and Canadian Foreign Minister Lawrence Cannon stated that "any militarization [of the Arctic] is out of the question." And in June 2011, then-Prime Minister (and currently President) Vladimir Putin stated, "Russia will definitely expand its presence in the Arctic. We are open for dialogue with our foreign partners and with all neighbors in the Arctic region. But we will naturally defend our own geopolitical interests firmly and consistently." The following month, Putin announced plans to build a large shipping port on the Yamal peninsula, and the government stated that it would be sending two brigades to the north to protect its interests.

Similarly, some Chinese leaders have voiced concern over perceived emerging security issues in the Arctic. In early March 2010, a Chinese admiral stated that "the current scramble for the sovereignty of the Arctic among some nations has encroached on many other countries' interests," and he added that China had to "make short and long term ocean strategic development plans to exploit the Arctic because it will become a future mission for the navy." Some analysts, however, believe that China's general approach toward the Arctic will remain decidedly low-key: "To date, China has adopted a wait-and-see approach to Arctic developments, wary that active overtures would cause alarm in other countries due to China's size and status as a rising global power." China is believed to be keen on resolving through diplomacy the national interests of both littoral and non-Arctic states in the high north. Toward that end, it has sought permanent observer status on the Arctic Council. However, its candidacy may be imperiled by a dispute with Norway, which in 2010 awarded the Nobel Peace Prize to Chinese dissident Liu Xiaobo. Norwegian political scientist Gunhild Hoogense Gjørv has noted that "[e]veryone is interested in the moves that China is making."[187]

As noted, the Arctic Council does not address regional security issues. To fill this apparent void, a recent report by the Center for Strategic and International Studies has proposed the creation of a separate organization, the Arctic Coast Guard Forum (ACGF), consisting initially of the eight Arctic Council states, but possibly expanding eventually to include other countries willing to contribute assets. The ACGF, which could potentially be headquartered at the U.S. Air Force base in Thule, Greenland, would "focus first on information sharing yet should also seek to develop methods of cooperation in support of the Arctic Council's search-and-rescue agreement and future international oil spill response agreement."[188]

U.S. Military Forces and Operations[189]

During the Cold War, the Arctic was an arena of military competition between the United States and the Soviet Union, with both countries, for example, operating nuclear-powered submarines,

---

[186] "Russia Will Protect Interests In Arctic: Official," *Agence France Presse,* June 10, 2009. "Russia Opposes Arms Race In Arctic Region—Diplomat," *ITAR-TASS World Service,* July 21, 2009.

[187] "China Prepares For An Ice-free Arctic," Linda Jakobson, *SIPRI Insights On Peace and Security*, No. 2010/2, March 2010. "Admiral Urges Government To Stake Claim In the Arctic," *South China Morning Post*, March 6, 2010. "Norway Wants to Block China from Arctic Council Over 2010 Nobel Peace Prize Row," *Agence France Presse,* January 25, 2012. "Clinton in Arctic to See Impact of Climate Change," *Agence France Presse,* June 2, 2012.

[188] "A New Security Architecture for the Arctic: An American Perspective," Center for Strategic and International Studies (CSIS), January 2012, p. 37.

[189] This section prepared by Ronald O'Rourke, Specialist in Naval Affairs, Foreign Affairs, Defense, and Trade Division.

---

long-range bombers, and tactical aircraft in the region.[190] The end of the Cold War and the collapse of most elements of the Russian military establishment following the dissolution of the Soviet Union in December 1991 greatly reduced this competition and led to a reduced emphasis on the Arctic in U.S. military planning.

The diminishment of Arctic sea ice is now leading U.S. military forces to pay renewed attention to the Arctic. This is particularly true in the case of the Navy and Coast Guard, for whom diminishment of Arctic sea ice is opening up potential new operating areas for their surface ships. Navy and Coast Guard activities relating to the Arctic are taking place as other countries, such as Canada, Russia, and Norway, are examining the potential implications for their military forces of diminished Arctic sea ice, and taking or contemplating steps to increase their own navy and coast guard presence and operations in the region.[191] Defense officials in the United States and other countries view issues such as sovereignty, freedom of navigation, and energy exploration as creating a potential in the Arctic for military cooperation, competition, or conflict, depending on how these issues are handled.[192]

DOD in General

2010 Quadrennial Defense Review

The Department of Defense's (DOD's) report on the 2010 Quadrennial Defense Review (QDR), submitted to Congress in February 2010, states:

> The effect of changing climate on the Department's operating environment is evident in the maritime commons of the Arctic. The opening of the Arctic waters in the decades ahead[,] which will permit seasonal commerce and transit[,] presents a unique opportunity to work collaboratively in multilateral forums to promote a balanced approach to improving human and environmental security in the region. In that effort, DoD must work with the Coast Guard and the Department of Homeland Security to address gaps in Arctic communications, domain awareness, search and rescue, and environmental observation and forecasting capabilities to support both current and future planning and operations. To support cooperative engagement in the Arctic, DoD strongly supports accession to the United Nations Convention on the Law of the Sea.[193]

The report also states:

---

[190] For a recent article concerning Soviet submarine operations in the Arctic during the Cold War, see Bob Weber, "Russian Maps Suggest Soviet Subs Cruised Canadian Arctic," *The Globe and Mail (www.theglobeandmail.com)*, December 6, 2011.

[191] See, for example, Associated Press, "Military Powers Beef Up Arctic Presence," *The Korea Times (www.koreatimes.co.kr)*, April 17, 2012, accessed June 15, 2012 at http://www.koreatimes.co.kr/www/news/tech/2012/ 06/129_109145.html; Alan Cullison, "Russia To Deploy Troops To Defend Interests In Arctic," *Wall Street Journal*, July 2, 2011: 2; David Pugliese, "[Canadian] Senators: Arm [Canadian] Coast Guard Patrols in Canada's Arctic," *Defense News*, January 18, 2010: 12.

[192] See, for example, John Vandiver, "NATO Commander Sees Arctic Seabed As Cooperative Zone," *Mideast Stars and Stripes*, October 10, 2009; Tom Coghlan, "Nato Commander Warns Of Conflict With Russia In Arctic Circle," *London Times*, October 3, 2009; Gerard O'Dwyer, "Danish Report: Conflicts Coming Over Arctic," *Defense News*, September 28, 2009: 18; Gerard O'Dwyer, "Russia Warns Denmark Over Arctic Arms Race," *Defense News*, August 3, 2009: 13; Gerrard Cowen, "Russia and NATO Look to Co-operation In Arctic," *Jane's Defence Weekly*, April 8, 2009: 12; David Scutro, "Thawing Arctic Seas May Bring Security Risk," *NavyTimes.com*, January 29, 2009.

[193] Department of Defense, *Quadrennial Defense Review Report*, February 2010, p. 86.

> The Department of Defense and its interagency partners must be able to more comprehensively monitor the air, land, maritime, space, and cyber domains for potential direct threats to the United States. Such monitoring provides the U.S. homeland with an extended, layered in depth defense. This effort includes enhanced coordination with Canada for the defense of North America as well as assisting Mexico and Caribbean partners in developing air and maritime domain awareness capacities. Special attention is required to develop domain awareness tools for the Arctic approaches as well. In coordination with domestic and international partners, DoD will explore technologies that have the potential to detect, track, and identify threats in these spheres to ensure that capabilities can be deployed to counter them in a timely fashion.[194]

The report further states:

> Central to the security of the United States is a strong transatlantic partnership, which is underpinned by the bilateral relationships between the United States and the governments of Europe. We will continue to work with this community of like-minded nations, whether by engaging with allies still shaping their democracies after decades of living in the shadow of the Soviet Union, building on the benefits of French reintegration into NATO's military structure, or addressing new security issues such as those arising in the Arctic region.[195]

The report states: "We will seek out opportunities to work with Moscow on emerging issues, such as the future of the Arctic" and that DOD "will also enhance defense relationships and continue to work with Canada in the context of regional security, increased interaction in the Arctic, and combat operations in Afghanistan."[196]

April 2011 Change to Unified Command Plan

In April 2011, it was reported that

> Changes made to the U.S. military's Unified Command Plan shift geographic boundaries and stress the growing importance of the Arctic, officials said.
>
> President Barack Obama signed the document yesterday [April 6].
>
> The biggest change to the plan assigns U.S. Northern Command responsibility for the Arctic. U.S. European Command and U.S. Pacific Command shared responsibility with U.S. Northern Command for the region under the last change published in December 2008. It also places responsibility for Alaska under Northern Command. The previous plan had Northern Command and U.S. Pacific Command sharing responsibility for the state and adjacent waters.
>
> "Northcom was given advocacy responsibility for Arctic capabilities primarily due to having the only U.S. Arctic territory within its area of operations," a Pentagon spokesman said.
>
> Northern Command also already works closely with Canada and "has a habitual relationship with the Department of Homeland Security and the U.S. Coast Guard," the spokesman continued. "These relationships are key to human and environmental safety and security."...

---

[194] Department of Defense, *Quadrennial Defense Review Report*, February 2010, p. 19.

[195] Department of Defense, *Quadrennial Defense Review Report*, February 2010, p. 57.

[196] Department of Defense, *Quadrennial Defense Review Report*, February 2010, p. 62.

The Unified Command Plan is the responsibility of the chairman of the Joint Chiefs of Staff, and is reviewed every two years. The Joint Staff coordinates input from the combatant commanders, the service chiefs and Defense Department leadership. The chairman, Navy Adm. Mike Mullen, submitted his recommendations through Defense Secretary Robert M. Gates to Obama.[197]

May 2011 Report to Congress

A May 2011 DOD report to Congress on Arctic operations and the Northwest Passage that was done at congressional direction[198] stated:

> The Arctic is warming on average twice as fast as the rest of the planet, resulting in increased human activity in the region. Although some perceive that competition for resources and boundary disputes may result in conflict in the Arctic, the opening of the Arctic also presents opportunities to work collaboratively in multilateral forums to promote a balanced approach to improving human and environmental security in the region.
>
> Strategic guidance on the Arctic is articulated in National Security Presidential Directive (NSPD) 66 / Homeland Security Presidential Directive (HSPD) 25, *Arctic Region Policy.* Additional guidance is found in *the 2010 National Security Strategy (NSS)* and the *2010 Quadrennial Defense Review (QDR).* The overarching strategic national security objective is *a stable and secure region where U.S. national interests are safeguarded and the U.S. homeland is protected.* This objective is consistent with a regional policy that reflects the relatively low level of threat in a region bounded by nation states that have not only publicly committed to working within a common framework of international law and diplomatic engagement, but also demonstrated ability and commitment to doing so over the last fifty years.
>
> DoD will take responsible steps to anticipate and prepare for the Arctic operations of the near-(2010-2020), mid- (2020-2030), and far-term (beyond 2030). Capabilities will need to be reevaluated as conditions change, and gaps must be addressed in order to be prepared to operate in a more accessible Arctic. Key challenges include: shortfalls in ice and weather reporting and forecasting; limitations in command, control, communications, computers, intelligence, surveillance, and reconnaissance (C4ISR) due to lack of assets and harsh

---

[197] Jim Garamone, "Unified Command Plan Reflects Arctic's Importance," *American Forces Press Service*, April 7, 2011.

[198] The direction was contained in the House Armed Services Committee's report (H.Rept. 111-491 of May 21, 2010) on H.R. 5136, the FY2011 National Defense Authorization Act, which stated that

> the committee directs the Secretary of Defense to submit a report to the congressional defense committees by May 30, 2011, that includes the following:
>
> (1) An assessment of the strategic national security objectives and restrictions in the Arctic Region;
>
> (2) An assessment on mission capabilities required to support the strategic national security objectives and a timeline to obtain such capabilities;
>
> (3) An assessment of an amended unified command plan that addresses opportunities of obtaining continuity of effort in the Arctic Ocean by a single combatant commander;
>
> (4) An assessment of the basing infrastructure required to support Arctic strategic objectives, including the need for a deep-water port in the Arctic; and
>
> (5) An assessment of the status of and need for icebreakers to determine whether icebreakers provide important or required mission capabilities to support Arctic strategic national security objectives, and an assessment of the minimum and optimal number of icebreakers that may be needed. (Page 337)

---

environmental conditions; limited inventory of ice-capable vessels; and limited shore-based infrastructure. The key will be to address needs in step with the rate at which activity in the Arctic increases, and balance potential investments in these capabilities with other national priorities. The United States has a vital Arctic neighbor and partner in Canada, with its shared values and interests in the region. DoD will work with the Canadian Department of National Defence (DND) to ensure common Arctic interests are addressed in a complementary manner.

Although having multiple Combatant Commanders (CCDRs) in the Arctic Ocean makes coordination more challenging, having too few would leave out key stakeholders, diminish longstanding relationships, and potentially alienate important partners. There are now two CCDRs with Arctic responsibilities: Commander, U.S. European Command (USEUCOM), and Commander, U.S. Northern Command (USNORTHCOM), each responsible for a portion of the Arctic Ocean aligned with adjacent land boundaries, an arrangement judged best suited to achieve continuity of effort with key regional partners.

Existing DoD posture in the region is adequate to meet near- to mid-term U.S. defense needs. DoD does not currently anticipate a need for the construction of a deep-draft port in Alaska between now and 2020. Given the long lead times for construction of major infrastructure in the region, DoD will periodically re-evaluate this assessment as the Combatant Commanders update their regional plans on a regular basis.

The United States needs assured Arctic access to support national interests in the Arctic. This access can be provided by a variety of proven capabilities, including submarines and aircraft, but only U.S.-flagged ice-capable ships provide visible U.S. sovereign maritime presence throughout the Arctic region. This need could potentially be met by either icebreakers or ice-strengthened surface vessels, none of which are in the U.S. Navy current surface combatant inventory, but which do exist in U.S. Coast Guard's inventory in limited numbers.

Finally, significant uncertainty remains about the rate and extent of climate change in the Arctic and the pace at which human activity will increase. The challenge is to balance the risk of being late-to-need with the opportunity cost of making premature Arctic investments. Not only does early investment take resources from other pressing needs, but the capabilities would be later in their lifecycle when finally employed. Given the many competing demands on DoD's resources in the current fiscal environment, the Department believes that further evaluation of the future operating environment is required before entertaining significant investments in infrastructure or capabilities.[199]

January 2012 GAO Report Reviewing May 2011 DOD Report

A January 2012, congressionally directed[200] GAO report reviewing the May 2011 DOD report above stated the following:

While DOD has undertaken some efforts to assess the capabilities needed to meet national security objectives in the Arctic, it is unclear whether DOD will be in a position to provide needed capabilities in a timely and efficient manner because it lacks a risk-based investment strategy for addressing near-term needs and a collaborative forum with the Coast Guard for

---

[199] Department of Defense, *Report to Congress on Arctic Operations and the Northwest Passage*, OUSD (Policy), May 2011. pp 2-4 (executive summary). See also Christopher J. Castelli, "Report: 'Significant' Gap Undermines DOD Tracking Of Ships In Arctic," *Inside the Pentagon*, June 16, 2011.

[200] The direction was contained on page 291 of in the House Armed Services Committee's report (H.Rept. 112-78 of May 17, 2011) on H.R. 1540, the FY2012 National Defense Authorization Act.

addressing long-term capability needs. DOD's [May 2011] Arctic Report acknowledges that it has some near-term gaps in key capabilities needed to communicate, navigate, and maintain awareness of activity in the region. However, DOD has not yet evaluated, selected, or implemented alternatives for prioritizing and addressing near-term Arctic capability needs. In addition, DOD and the Coast Guard have established a working group to identify potential collaborative efforts to enhance U.S. Arctic capabilities. This working group is focused on identifying potential near-term investments but not longer-term needs, and it is currently expected to be dissolved in January 2012. Uncertainty involving the rate of Arctic climate change necessitates careful planning to ensure efficient use of resources in developing Arctic needs such as basing infrastructure and icebreakers, which require long lead times to develop and are expensive to build and maintain. Without taking steps to meet near- and long-term Arctic capability needs, DOD risks making premature Arctic investments, being late in obtaining needed capabilities, or missing opportunities to minimize costs by collaborating on investments with the Coast Guard....

DOD has several efforts under way to assess the capabilities needed to support U.S. strategic objectives in the Arctic. However, it has not yet developed a comprehensive approach to addressing Arctic capabilities that would include steps such as developing a risk-based investment strategy and timeline to address near-term needs and establishing a collaborative forum with the Coast Guard to identify long-term Arctic investments....

According to DOD's Arctic Report, capabilities will need to be reassessed as conditions change, and gaps will need to be addressed to be prepared to operate in a more accessible Arctic. Other stakeholders have also assessed Arctic capability gaps. Examples of these efforts include the following:

- U.S. Northern Command initiated a commander's estimate for the Arctic in December 2010 that, according to officials, will establish the commander's intent and missions in the Arctic and identify capability shortfalls. In addition, Northern Command identified two Arctic-specific capability gaps (communications and maritime domain awareness) in its fiscal years 2013 through 2017 integrated priority list, which defines the combatant command's highest-priority capability gaps for the near-term, including shortfalls that may adversely affect missions.

- U.S. European Command completed an Arctic Strategic Assessment in April 2011 that, among other things, identified Arctic capability gaps in the areas of environmental protection, maritime domain awareness, cooperative development of environmental awareness technology, sharing of environmental data, and lessons learned on infrastructure development. In addition, it recommended that the command conduct a more detailed mission analysis for potential Arctic missions, complete a detailed capability estimate for Arctic operations, and work in conjunction with Northern Command and the Departments of the Navy and Air Force to conduct a comprehensive capabilities-based assessment for the Arctic.

- DOD and DHS established the Capabilities Assessment Working Group (working group) in May 2011 to identify shared Arctic capability gaps as well as opportunities and approaches to overcome them, to include making recommendations for near-term investments. The working group was directed by its Terms of Reference to focus on four primary capability areas when identifying potential collaborative efforts to enhance Arctic capabilities, including near-term investments. Those capability areas include maritime domain awareness, communications, infrastructure, and presence. The working group was also directed to identify overlaps and redundancies in established and emerging DOD and DHS Arctic requirements. As the advocate for Arctic capabilities, Northern Command was assigned lead responsibility for DOD in the working group, while the Coast Guard was assigned lead responsibility for DHS. The establishment of the working group—which, among other things, is to identify opportunities for bi-departmental action to close Arctic capability gaps and issue recommendations for near-term investments—helps to ensure that collaboration between the Coast Guard and DOD is taking place to identify near-term capabilities needed to support current planning and operations. Although the working group is developing a paper with its recommendations, officials indicated that additional assessments would be required to address those recommendations.

- U.S. Navy completed its first Arctic capabilities-based assessment in September 2011 and is developing a second capabilities-based assessment focused on observing, mapping, and environmental prediction capabilities in the Arctic, which officials expect to be completed in the spring of 2012. The Navy's first Arctic capabilities-based assessment identified three critical capability gaps as the highest priorities, including the capabilities to provide environmental information; maneuver safely on the sea surface; and conduct training, exercise, and education. This assessment recommended several near-term actions to address these gaps....

Even though DOD has made preliminary efforts to identify Arctic capability gaps and assess strategic objectives, constraints, and risks in the Arctic, DOD has not yet evaluated, selected, or implemented alternatives for prioritizing and addressing near-term Arctic capability needs....

Given that the opening in the Arctic presents a wide range of challenges for DOD, a risk-based investment strategy and timeline can help DOD develop the capabilities needed to meet national security interests in the region. Without a risk-based investment strategy and timeline for prioritizing and addressing near-term Arctic capability gaps and challenges, which is periodically updated to reflect evolving needs, DOD could be slow to develop needed capabilities, potentially facing operational risk and higher costs if the need arises to execute plans rapidly. Conversely, DOD could move too early, making premature Arctic investments that take resources from other, more pressing needs or producing capabilities that could be outdated before they are used.

While DOD and DHS have established the working group to identify shared near-term Arctic capability gaps, this collaborative forum is not intended to address long-term Arctic capability gaps or identify opportunities for joint investments over the longer-term. DOD acknowledged the importance of collaboration with the Coast Guard over the long-term in its 2010 Quadrennial Defense Review, which states that the department must work with the Coast Guard and DHS to develop Arctic capabilities to support both current and future planning and operations. According to DOD and Coast Guard officials, although the working group is primarily focused on near-term investments, it has discussed some mid- to long-term capability needs. However, DOD and Coast Guard officials stated that after the completion of the working group's paper, expected in January 2012, the working group will have completed the tasks detailed in the Terms of Reference and will be dissolved. Consequently, no forum will exist to further address any mid- to long-term capability needs....

After the working group completes its tasks in January 2012, there will be no DOD and Coast Guard organization focused specifically on reducing overlap and redundancies or collaborating to address Arctic capability gaps in support of future planning and operations, as is directed by the 2010 Quadrennial Defense Review.

While Northern Command officials stated they have plans for periodic reassessment of long-term capability needs, such as icebreakers or basing infrastructure including a deep-water port, it is not clear how those plans consider collaboration with the Coast Guard. For example, officials stated the biennial review of Northern Command's Theater Campaign

Plan and Strategic Infrastructure Master Plan will consider long-term capability and infrastructure needs. They added that the commander's Arctic Estimate is reviewed annually and also considers long-term priorities, such as identifying a need for icebreakers. However, the officials stated that the Arctic Estimate does not identify how DOD would acquire those icebreakers or how it would coordinate with the Coast Guard—the operator of the nation's icebreakers—to reconstruct existing or build new icebreakers....

Without specific plans for a collaborative forum between DOD and the Coast Guard to address long-term Arctic capability gaps and to identify opportunities for joint investments over the longer-term, DOD may miss opportunities to leverage resources with the Coast Guard to enhance future Arctic capabilities.

At this time, significant DOD investments in Arctic capabilities may not be needed, but that does not preclude taking steps to anticipate and prepare for Arctic operations in the future. Addressing near-term gaps is essential for DOD to have the key enabling capabilities it needs to communicate, navigate, and maintain awareness of activity in the region. An investment strategy that identifies and prioritizes near-term Arctic capability needs and identifies a timeline to address them would be useful for decision makers in planning and budgeting. Without taking deliberate steps to analyze risks in the Arctic and prioritize related resource and operational requirements, DOD could later find itself faced with urgent needs, resulting in higher costs that could have been avoided.

In addition, unless DOD and DHS continue to collaborate to identify opportunities for interagency action to close Arctic capability gaps, DOD could miss out on opportunities to work with the Coast Guard to leverage resources for shared needs. DOD may choose to create a new collaborative forum or incorporate this collaboration into an existing forum or process. Given the different missions and associated timelines of DOD and the Coast Guard for developing Arctic capabilities, it is important that the two agencies work together to avoid fragmented efforts and reduce unaffordable overlap and redundancies while addressing Arctic capability gaps in support of future planning and operations.

To more effectively leverage federal investments in Arctic capabilities in a resource-constrained environment and ensure needed capabilities are developed in a timely way, we recommend that the Secretary of Defense, in consultation with the Secretary of the Department of Homeland Security, take the following two actions:

- develop a risk-based investment strategy that: 1) identifies and prioritizes near-term Arctic capability needs, 2) develops a timeline for addressing them, and 3) is updated as appropriate; and

- establish a collaborative forum with the Coast Guard to fully leverage federal investments and help avoid overlap and redundancies in addressing long-term Arctic capability needs.

In written comments on a draft of this report, DHS concurred with both of our recommendations. For its part, DOD partially concurred with both of our recommendations. It generally agreed that the department needed to take action to address the issues we raised but indicated it is already taking initial steps to address them.[201]

---

[201] Government Accountability Office, Arctic Capabilities[:]DOD Addressed Many Specified Reporting Elements in Its 2011 Arctic Report but Should Take Steps to Meet Near- and Long-term Needs, GAO-12-180, January 2012, Summary page and pp. 12-18.

June 2012 Senate Armed Services Committee Report Language

The Senate Armed Services Committee, in its report (S.Rept. 112-173 of June 4, 2012) on S. 3254, the FY2013 National Defense Authorization Act, stated:

Arctic region

The committee recognizes the continued importance of the Arctic region to our broader national strategy. Declining ice cover continues to open the Arctic region and a concerted, systematic, and immediate effort should be undertaken to adequately protect the United States' security, environmental, energy, economic, and natural resource interests in the Arctic.

The committee commends the Department of Defense (DOD) and, in particular, U.S. Northern Command and the Department of the Navy, and other federal agencies, such as the Department of Homeland Security (DHS), through the U.S. Coast Guard, the Department of Commerce, through the National Oceanic and Atmospheric Administration and the U.S. Arctic Research Commission, for their progress thus far in studying the region and defining the capabilities required to effectively operate in and protect the domain.

International and interagency collaboration is also needed to develop the necessary mapping and charting resources required for safe navigation and to promote security and economic interests. As sea ice recedes, timely weather forecasts and disaster warnings along with more baseline data will be required to conduct successful search and rescue missions. Search and rescue coordination, planning, and training for the Arctic should be thoroughly analyzed and developed to ensure forces can successfully operate in the domain.

The committee recognizes the importance of DOD's involvement in interagency and international efforts to protect national security interests in the region and, accordingly, urges DOD to continue to work in concert with DHS to establish a formal chartered working group to pursue increasing Arctic capabilities in the areas of communications, maritime domain awareness, infrastructure, and presence, as was recommended by U.S. Northern Command and the U.S. Coast Guard in a joint White Paper dated March 13, 2012. The committee also urges the agencies to develop an investment strategy for funding emerging requirements in balance with a resource constrained environment. (Pages 194-195)

Navy and Coast Guard

The Navy and Coast Guard are exploring the potential implications that increased surface ship and aircraft operations in the Arctic may have for required numbers of ships and aircraft, ship and aircraft characteristics, new or enlarged Arctic bases, and supporting systems, such as navigation and communication systems. The Navy and Coast Guard have sponsored or participated in studies and conferences to explore these implications, the Coast Guard has deployed boats and aircraft into the region to better understand the implications of operating such units there,[202] and

---

[202] See Susan Gvozdas, "U.S. Coast Guard Preps For Open Arctic Waters," *Defense News*, September 7, 2009: 40; John C. Marcario, "Return to the Arctic," Seapower, August 2009: 26-27; John C. Marcario, "Coming Into Focus," Seapower, March 2009: 42, 44; John C. Marcario, "Arctic Presence," Seapower, August 2008: 32-33; Emelie Rutherford, "Coast Guard To Test How Ships and Aircraft Operate in Arctic," *Inside the Navy*, January 21, 2008; Philip Ewiing, "Allen: CG Expedition To Assess Arctic Waters," *NavyTimes.com*, January 17, 2009; Patricia Kime, "North Pole Flyover A First For Coast Guard," *NavyTimes.com*, October 25, 2007.

Navy sailors in 2009 rode on Canadian Navy ships deploying to Arctic waters for similar reasons.[203]

Points or themes that have emerged in studies and conferences regarding the potential implications for the U.S. Navy and Coast Guard of diminished Arctic sea ice include but are not limited to the following:

- The diminishment of Arctic ice is creating potential new operating areas in the Arctic for Navy surface ships and Coast Guard cutters.

- U.S. national security interests in the Arctic include "such matters as missile defense and early warning; deployment of sea and air systems for strategic sealift, strategic deterrence, maritime presence, and maritime security operations; and ensuring freedom of navigation and overflight."[204]

- A mission of potential particular interest for expanded surface ship operations in the Arctic would be defending the U.S. (and European Union) claim that the Northern Sea Route running along Russia's north coast and the Northwest Passage running through Canada's northern archipelago constitute international straits which allow right of innocent passage.

- Search and rescue in the Arctic is a mission of increasing importance, particularly for the Coast Guard, and one that poses potentially significant operational challenges (see "Search and Rescue" above).

- More complete and detailed information on the Arctic is needed to more properly support expanded Navy and Coast Guard ship and aircraft operations in the Arctic.

- The Navy and the Coast Guard currently have limited infrastructure in place in the Arctic to support expanded ship and aircraft operations in the Arctic.[205]

---

[203] Andrew Scutro, "Navy Preps For Uncharted Arctic Waters," *NavyTimes.com*, November 24, 2009.

[204] NSPD 66/HSPD 25, Section III B.

[205] Regarding infrastructure in the Arctic, an October 2009 press report stated:

> A big challenge will be logistics support since the only [U.S.] supply base currently available is the town of Barrow, Alaska. [Rear Admiral Dave] Titley [the Oceanographer of the Navy] explained that the Arctic region is roughly the size of the United States. By way of illustration Titley said: "Think of trying to conduct operations through the entire U.S., and your one logistics base is the size of San Clemente Island [an island off the coast of Southern California]. That is roughly the size of Barrow."

(Bob Freeman, "Conference Addresses Navy's Role in a Changing Arctic," Navy New Service, October 4, 2009. See also Zachary M. Peterson, "As A Result of Melting Ice, Navy Study Need For Base in Far North," *Inside the Navy*, December 29, 2009; Patricia Kime, "CG Boss Calls For Forward Bases In The Arctic," *NavyTimes.com*, September 28, 2007.)

- Expanded ship and aircraft operations in the Arctic may require altering ship and aircraft designs and operating methods.[206]

- Cooperation with other Arctic countries will be valuable in achieving defense and homeland security goals.

Navy in General

In a February 2009 journal article, the Oceanographer of the Navy stated:

> Competing claims dealing with the Arctic are often political in nature and have important implications. For example, in the summer of 2008 Canada announced that it would increase its military presence in the region, begin construction of a deep-water port on Baffin Island, establish a cold weather training base at Resolute Bay, and build six new ice-hardened ships to patrol the Northwest Passage. During the same period, Russia conducted strategic bomber flights over the area for the first time since the end of the Cold War....

> Preserving freedom of navigation in the region is an important tenet of U.S. policy. The NSR [Northern Sea Route], however, is a contested waterway, with Russian claims of sovereignty competing against U.S. and European Union insistence that it is an international strait available to all nations, subject to mutually recognized terms. Another potential [Arctic] transoceanic shipping route may be the Northwest Passage, which extends from the Atlantic through Baffin Bay and the Canadian Archipelago and into the Pacific by way of the Bering Strait. Canada claims sovereignty over the waters of the Canadian Archipelago, although the United States and the European Union claim that the Northwest Passage also constitutes an international strait which allows right of innocent passage....

> Aside from access and right of passage, the Navy and Coast Guard, in particular, must also be concerned with strategic choke points such as the Bering Strait, Canada's Queen Elizabeth Islands in the Northwest Passage, and Russia's Severnaya Zemlya and New Siberian Islands in the Northern Sea Route. These narrow passages offer some protection from persistent ice blockage, but they are also vulnerable to control or blockade by adversaries that would significantly disrupt potential commercial shipping and oil transport....

> U.S. naval interests will face new challenges in an increasingly ice-free Arctic with a strategic objective to understand potential threats to the United States from the maritime domain. As throughout the global commons, the U.S. Navy must be aware of activities that could be harmful to national security interests in a region that will, no doubt, see fewer barriers to access by potential adversaries in the future. National and homeland security interests pertinent to the U.S. Navy in the region would include early warning/missile defense; maritime presence and security; and freedom of navigation and over-flight....

> The region is primarily a maritime domain and the U.S. Navy of the future must be prepared to protect sea lines of communication supporting maritime commerce and other national interests—including national security—there. In addition to thinking through how we adjust

[206] For articles discussing potential changes to ship and aircraft designs, see Dan Taylor, "Roughead: Navy Will Have To Design Ships To Better Handle Arctic," *Inside the Navy*, November 26, 2009; Rebekah Gordon, "Coast Guard OPC [Offshore Patrol Cutter] Modifications For Varied Environments A Possibility," *Inside the Navy*, August 24, 2009; Andrew Scutro, "Arctic Forces Fleet to Look North," *NavyTimes.com*, February 23, 2009; Amy McCullough, "Stronger Hulls Could Help Fill Icebreaker Gap," *NavyTimes.com*, February 22, 2009; Rebekah Gordon, "Coast Guard Evaluating Effects of Increased Arctic Operations on Fleet," Inside the Navy, February 9, 2009.

our shipbuilding emphasis to support such operations, the Navy should also be thinking strategically about building the necessary infrastructure to provide logistic support for Arctic patrols, search and rescue capabilities, and shore-based support activities.

To ensure complete maritime domain awareness in the region, and to provide our forces a competitive advantage, it will be necessary to have comprehensive knowledge of the physical environment. Data must be obtained by a suite of remote sensors (satellites, radars), autonomous sensors (data buoys, unmanned vehicles), and manned sensors (shipboard, coastal observing stations). Computer-based ocean and atmospheric models must be adjusted to the geophysical peculiarities of high latitudes. Communication lines for data exchange and reach-back processing at high-performance computing production centers must be robust and reliable. To ensure safety of navigation, we will also need to conduct more high-resolution bottom surveys and increase the scrutiny we place on sea ice conditions.

The Navy relies on its international and interagency partners for assistance to ensure success of maritime domain awareness and maritime security missions. To meet the demands of national security in the changing northern environment, strengthening mechanisms for cooperation among the regional nations and U.S. agencies must remain a high priority. Like everywhere else in the world, sound national security in the Arctic will require strategic access, military mobility, safe navigation, unimpeded maritime transportation, improved homeland security, and responsible, sustainable use of ocean and coastal resources. International and interagency agreements and partnerships are vital to incorporating these essential elements into a viable national security policy and will be critical for resolving future naval challenges of a changing Arctic.[207]

In a spring 2010 journal article, the Oceanographer of the Navy (the successor to the officer who authored the above journal article) and a coauthor stated that "Navy surface vessels are able to operate up to the marginal ice zone but will require ice-strengthening to operate in higher ice conditions; Navy aircraft are capable of operating in the Arctic, but the lack of divert fields limits their duration and range."[208] The article also stated:

While the Navy has a rich history in the Arctic, several challenges must be met to ensure successful operations in the future. These include the lack of support infrastructure and logistics support, environmental hazards such as drifting sea ice and icing on exposed surfaces, and communications difficulties. Antiquated nautical charts, drifting ice, low visibility, and the paucity of electronic and visual navigation aids hinder safety of navigation. A lack of coastal installations also contributes to the difficulty of search and rescue (SAR) operations. The only American-owned deepwater port near the Arctic basin is Dutch Harbor, in the Aleutian Islands.[209]

A March 2010 press report stated that

a sustained [Navy] presence [in the Arctic] requires a lot of answers and training in the near future. Specifically, the harsh environment will require significant modifications in ship and satellite architecture.

---

[207] David Grove, "Arctic Melt: Reopening a Naval Frontier?" *U.S. Naval Institute Proceedings*, February 2009: 16-21.

[208] David W. Titley and Courtney C. St. John, "Arctic Security Considerations and the U.S. Navy's Roadmap for the Arctic," *Naval War College Review*, Spring 2010: 41.

[209] David W. Titley and Courtney C. St. John, "Arctic Security Considerations and the U.S. Navy's Roadmap for the Arctic," *Naval War College Review*, Spring 2010: 42.

"Where do we keep our fuel?" [Admiral Gary Roughead] the CNO [Chief of Naval Operations] said. "The way that we design our heating and ventilation systems are just not designed to keep up with ambient temperatures that are as cold as it gets up there. You have difficulties sometimes in how the more traditional outside equipment is maintained, and when you have freezing rain and things like that, how do you keep it clear? There are a lot of ship designs and ship alterations aspects. ... What sort of communication architectures do we have to have? I really believe now is the time to start thinking about that because it means changes to ship design, which means we have to start laying in. It means perhaps some new overhead satellite architectures, and those are extraordinarily costly."[210]

On June 16, 2011, in remarks at a seminar on the Arctic, Admiral Gary Roughead, the Chief of Naval Operations, stated:

Well in my mind, there is a phenomenal event taking place on the planet today, and that is what I call the opening of the Fifth Ocean; that's the Arctic Ocean. We haven't had an ocean open on this planet since the end of the Ice Age. So if this is not a significant change that requires new, and I would submit, brave thinking on the topic, I don't know what other sort of physical event could produce that.

We in the Navy a couple of years ago began to look at how we as a Navy serve the nation.... So as we began to look at the planet, we realized that there were significant changes taking place; opening of the Fifth Ocean; physical changes; changes in population as they compressed into the littoral areas.

And so we established, I established something that I call Task Force Climate Change. Primarily focused on the Arctic because of the massive changes that are taking place up there, but it also takes into account what is happening on the rest of the planet and where we as a Navy think we have to be in the future. And then from that Task Force Climate Change, we developed what we call the Arctic road map....

The way we see things taking place is the first of moves, which will largely be in the area of resources. Fishing stocks will move with the water temperature, they will start to drift farther north, that will take fishing fleets farther north and there is a set of responsibilities that we have with other nations on making sure that that activity is taking place lawfully.

Then we believe the next step will be the extraction of resources. So what do we have to be prepared to do as a Navy, as a military particularly aligned closely with the Coast Guard on this.

And then in about 20 years time, 25 years time, the Arctic becomes a profitable sea route from Asia to Europe over the top of the planet. If you look at some of the estimates from shippers, some may actually be here. That is about a million dollars a trip someone saves. That is not insignificant. And so it will become a busy place as transportation starts to take place. That is how we envision the changes that are taking place, how we are looking at them, and the road map that we put in place is based on the best science as we know today. And we are committed to providing the resources the nation needs from the naval perspective to meet our needs.[211]

---

[210] Lance M. Bacon, "Ice Breaker," *Armed Forces Journal*, March 2010: 16-19, 34-35.

[211] Source: Text of remarks of Chief of Naval Operations Admiral Gary Roughead at Active in the Arctic Seminar, June 16, 2011.

Four days later, in remarks to a symposium on the impacts on naval and maritime operations of an ice-diminishing Arctic, Admiral Roughead stated:

> Since this forum began in 2001, our Navy has benefitted from the development and the discussion of the Arctic Symposium, as it has improved our appreciation greatly for an ice-diminished Arctic and the security implications that will follow from that physical change that will take place.
>
> This broader examination is something that we've endeavored to focus on systematically since we stood up our Task Force Climate Change in May 2009, and issued our Arctic Roadmap that same year. And rather than all the answers, what our efforts have given us is an appreciation of just how dynamic the study of the region is and surely will be in the future....
>
> ... at a fundamental level, the trends point undeniably towards a new venue of operations and responsibility for our global Navy – for preserving American interests in free and fair access there – and in light of this we remain committed to preparing exhaustively for the challenges and especially for the opportunities that are going to exist in an ice-diminishing Arctic.
>
> The U.S. Navy's interests in the Arctic are not new, of course. We have many decades of experience with exploration and, indeed, episodic operations in the waters of the Arctic Circle....
>
> But never has our interest encountered the confluence of trends, as projected by the U.S. Geological Survey in 2008 and the National Research Council this past March, that promises to change the Arctic so pervasively, and in so doing affect the global environment for which we plan and program our future fleet....
>
> In projecting the impact of climate change in the northern latitudes, however, I'm reminded of what Dr. Lubchenco observed just this past March, when she said, "what happens in the Arctic does not stay there." The trends we discuss here, in a similar timeframe, promise more disruption and disorder in a world whose population is growing rapidly, and moving to megacities on or near the coasts of almost every continent. The prospects of sea level rise, for some megacities, or the coral islands of the Maldives, are similarly daunting. We also have to consider the likely frictions that arise as fishing stocks migrate with changing sea temperatures, and the very real possibility that conflicts in the future will be fought over access to dwindling natural supplies of fresh water.
>
> It is because of these projections that our Navy is preparing for increased demand, both in the region - where we will maintain our access and uphold the freedom of navigation as a global good - and beyond, where we expect developments to expose the costs of our national reluctance on the Law of the Sea convention and to test our present understanding of customary legal guarantees to the very freedoms behind our global operations today. We are considering the technical requirements for polar operations to support our strategic objective of a safe, stable, and secure Arctic region where our national interests are safeguarded – namely, how and when to build forces capable and competent for the harsh northern climes.
>
> We also remain well aware of how important maritime partnerships will be in addressing capacity concerns as we seek to reinforce universal values in the global commons. Some speak of a changing Arctic in terms of either a race or a zero-sum game. As far as the U.S. Navy is concerned, it is neither. Rather, we see it as an opportunity to extend to the 'Fifth Ocean' the principles that have benefitted all peaceful nations in the other four. Secretary of State Clinton's attendance at the meeting of Arctic Council ministers last month in Nuuk, Greenland, signals the United States" level of interest in the region, as well as our belief in the power of international cooperation to advance mutual interests in the free use of the

maritime domain. It was also inherently practical in that it forged the much-needed agreement among Arctic states to improve our coordination on search and rescue.

As we stated in our Arctic Roadmap, the Navy will continue to pursue cooperative relationships around such areas of common interest, whether mission enablers like Maritime Domain Awareness, core naval capabilities such as humanitarian assistance and disaster response, or intra-governmental relationships like defense support to civil authorities. Exercises such as the Canadian Navy's 'Operation Nanook,' which we observed in 2009 and had the privilege of participating in last August alongside our Coast Guard counterparts, enhance our preparedness in several of these areas, and lay the basis from which we might extend the same maritime partnership and interoperability we have come to value so highly in our global operations. Joint exercises such as the U.S. Pacific Command's 'Northern Edge' – which started just outside of the Arctic Circle one week ago today and will continue throughout this week – ensure that we as a Navy remain ready to partner at the high end of operations as required.[212]

An April 28, 2012, press report states:

As global warming opens the Arctic Ocean to commercial and industrial traffic, the U.S. Navy is pushing to catch up with Russia, Canada and even Denmark in its Arctic ability. If a crisis were to happen now, the Navy lacks the ability to act in the Arctic without the help of one of those countries or the Coast Guard.

Last year, the Navy asked the War Gaming Department of the U.S. Naval War College to find out what the Navy needs for sustained operations in the Arctic.

In the resulting 2011 Fleet Arctic Operations Game, the Navy learned how big its Arctic shortcomings are. As a force, the Navy lacks everything from bases and Arctic-capable ships to reliable communications and cold-weather clothing....

The game's conclusions: the Navy is not adequately prepared to conduct long-term maritime Arctic operations; Arctic weather conditions increase the risk of failure; and most critically, to operate in the Arctic, the Navy will need to lean on the U.S. Coast Guard, countries like Russia or Canada, or tribal and industrial partners.

To sustain operations in the Arctic, the Navy needs ice-capable equipment, accurate and timely environmental data, personnel trained to operate in extreme weather, and better communications systems. Much of the environmental data will come from other Arctic nations....

Navy officials understand the need to conduct exercises in the Arctic so they can get ready for the real thing, but they don't have a strategy.

"We are the only Arctic nation without an Arctic strategy," said U.S. Navy Cmdr. Blake McBride, Arctic Affairs officer for Task Force Climate Change. "The Coast Guard and Department of Defense are working on a strategy to help answer the issue, and advocate for capabilities."

---

[212] Source: Text of remarks of Chief of Naval Operations Admiral Gary Roughead at the 4th Symposium on the Impacts of an Ice-Diminishing Arctic on Naval & Maritime Operations, June 20, 2011. See also Christopher J. Castelli, "Roughead: International Approach Needed To Fix Arctic-Awareness Gap," *Inside the Navy*, June 27, 2011.

Aside from signing National Security Presidential Directive 66, which requires the U.S. to have a presence in the Arctic, the Arctic hasn't been a priority for the U.S. government, largely because there isn't an immediate military threat.

"It's becoming a higher priority, but we don't make our own priorities," McBride said. "We don't foresee a military threat in the Arctic, but it doesn't mean we will not need to be able to operate there."

The Navy's future plans to conduct operations in the Arctic largely depend on the budget.

"It's all about the money," McBride said. "If you don't have the budget or funds to invest in manpower and equipment then you don't have anything."[213]

2009 Navy Arctic Roadmap

The Navy examined issues and concerns relating to climate change at a May 15, 2009, meeting of the Chief of Naval Operations (CNO) Executive Board. Following this meeting, the Navy decided to establish a Navy group led by the Oceanographer of the Navy called Task Force Climate Change (TFCC), and to develop Navy roadmaps first for the Arctic, and later for more general responses to global climate change.

The Navy issued its Arctic roadmap on November 10, 2009.[214] The document, which is dated October 2009 and co-sponsored by TFCC and the Oceanographer of the Navy,[215] is intended to guide the service's activities regarding the Arctic for the period FY2010-FY2014. The November 10 cover memo states that the document is to remain in effect until the completion of the report on the FY2014 Quadrennial Defense Review (QDR), at which time it will be reviewed and revised to incorporate guidance from that QDR.

The roadmap states that "significant action items" for FY2010 for the Navy included the following:

- Conduct assessments of fleet readiness and mission requirements in the Arctic region.
- Develop Navy strategic objectives in the Arctic region.
- Continue partnership-building activities with stakeholders in the region and conduct a limited objective experiment (or LOE—a kind of exercise) for the Arctic.
- Continue monitoring the Air Force's Polar Military Satellite Communications (MILSTACOM) program.
- Advocate for U.S. accession to the U.N. Convention on the Law of the Sea.

---

[213] Nicole Klauss, "War Games Find U.S. Navy Ability Lacking In Acrtic," *Fairbanks Daily News-Miner*, April 28, 2012.

[214] Memorandum for Distribution dated November 10, 2009, from Admiral J. W. Greenert, Vice Chief of Naval Operations, on the subject of the Navy Arctic Roadmap. The document was posted on *InsideDefense.com* (subscription required).

[215] U.S. Navy, U.S. Navy Arctic Roadmap, Washington, 2009, 29 pp. (October 2009, sponsored by Task Force Climate Change [and] Oceanographer of the Navy.) The document was posted on *InsideDefense.com* (subscription required).

- Develop a Navy position regarding combatant commander authorities and responsibilities for the Arctic.

- Conduct research and development on a next-generation environmental prediction capability that is applicable to the Arctic.

The roadmap states that "significant action items" for FY2011-FY2012 for the Navy include the following:

- Initiate assessments of required Navy Arctic capabilities.

- Develop recommendations to address Arctic requirements for program proposals in the Navy's Program Objective Memorandum (or POM—a document that guides the development of a Navy budget) for FY2014 (POM-14).

- Continue biennial Navy participation in Arctic exercises, including ICEX-11, ICEX-13, Arctic Edge, and Arctic Care.

- Formalize new cooperative relationships that increase Navy experience and competency in search and rescue (SAR), maritime domain awareness (MDA), and humanitarian assistance and disaster response (HADR) in the Arctic, and defense support of civil authorities (DSCA) in Alaska.

The roadmap states that "significant action items" for FY2013-FY2014 for the Navy include the following:

- Execute Navy POM-14 budget initiatives that address Arctic requirements.

- Initiate combined (i.e., multi-lateral) and bilateral activities which support safety, security, and stability in the region.[216]

A January 2011 press report stated that

> Two studies that will define the new assets the Navy will need to operate in the Arctic and what those operations will look like are "nearing completion," according to Rear Adm. David Titley, the oceanographer of the Navy, who spoke with Inside the Navy in a Jan. 18 interview.

> The studies, called the Capabilities Based Assessment and the Mission Analysis, were both called for in the Navy's 2009 Arctic Roadmap, a strategic document meant to guide the service's efforts in the Arctic. The capabilities assessment will undergo a flag officer review within the next month, according to Titley.[217]

Another January 2011 press report stated:

> The Navy has decided to re-establish the Office of Naval Research's [ONR's] Arctic program as part of an increasing focus on the region, according to Navy officials....

---

[216] For additional discussion of the roadmap, see David W. Titley and Courtney C. St. John, "Arctic Security Considerations and the U.S. Navy's Roadmap for the Arctic," *Naval War College Review*, Spring 2010: 35-48.

[217] Andrew Burt, "Navy Studies On Mission, Capability Needs For Arctic 'Nearing Completion'," *Inside the Navy*, January 21, 2011.

In 2009, the Navy's Arctic Roadmap laid out the service's strategy for the region, stating that by the fourth quarter of fiscal year 2011 the Navy would "evaluate the re-establishment of ONR's High Latitude Program" to study the Arctic.

In August 2011, the Navy released an Arctic environment assessment and outlook report.[218] The report states that it

> addresses Action Item 5.7 of the U.S. Navy Arctic Roadmap - to produce an Arctic Environmental Assessment and Outlook Report. This first biennial report provides a comprehensive assessment of the state of the Arctic environment, including the oceanography, hydrography, meteorology, fisheries, ice-extent, and climatic trends. This is important because the IPCC [reporting] refresh rate is too long to meet the budget POM [Program Objective Memorandum] cycle,[219] so this assessment will periodically synthesize existing scientific reports to inform POMs, specifically POM-[FY20]14; this allows the Navy's decisions to be based on sound science, and not use one source only, but a consensus of accepted sources....

> As the Arctic environment continues to change and human activity increases, the U.S. Navy must be prepared to operate in this region. It is important to note that even though the Arctic is opening up, it will continue to be a harsh and challenging environment for the foreseeable future due to hazardous sea ice, freezing temperatures and extreme weather. Although the Navy submarine fleet has decades of experience operating in the Arctic, the surface fleet, air assets, and U.S. Marine Corps ground troops have limited experience there. The Navy must now consider the Arctic in terms of future policy, strategy, force structure, and investments.[220]

An April 28, 2012, press report states:

> Navy officials have done the work called for in phase one and two of the [Arctic] roadmap, which largely consisted of developing research, assessing fleet readiness, completing capabilities-based assessments like the Fleet Arctic Operations Game, and formalizing cooperative agreements.

> The biggest hurdle comes in the next phase, which calls for funding equipment and Arctic training. Navy officials say they are drafting a budget request to address those items.[221]

September 2010 GAO Report on Coast Guard's Arctic Requirements

A September 2010 GAO report on the Coast Guard's efforts to identify Arctic requirements in general stated:

> The Coast Guard has taken specific action to identify Arctic requirements and gaps while also collecting relevant information from routine operations. The High Latitude Study is the centerpiece of the agency's efforts to determine its Arctic requirements. The Coast Guard has

---

[218] Department of the Navy, *Arctic Environmental Assessment and Outlook Report*, August 2011, 25 pp. Accessed at http://greenfleet.dodlive.mil/files/2011/08/U.S.-Navy-Arctic-Environmental-Assessment.pdf.

[219] The POM is an internal DOD document that guides the development of DOD's annual budget submissions to Congress.

[220] Department of the Navy, *Arctic Environmental Assessment and Outlook Report*, August 2011, p. v.

[221] Nicole Klauss, "War Games Find U.S. Navy Ability Lacking In Acrtic," *Fairbanks Daily News-Miner*, April 28, 2012.

also established temporary operating locations in the Arctic and conducted biweekly Arctic overflights to obtain more information on the Arctic operating environment. In addition, information gathered during the Coast Guard's routine missions—ice breaking, search and rescue, and others—also informs requirements. The agency's preliminary efforts to identify its Arctic requirements generally align with key practices for agencies defining missions and desired outcomes.

The Coast Guard faces Arctic challenges including limited information, minimal assets and infrastructure, personnel issues, and difficult planning and funding decisions, but is taking initial steps to address these challenges. Specifically, the Coast Guard does not currently have Arctic maritime domain awareness—a full understanding of variables that could affect the security, safety, economy, or environment in the Arctic—but is acquiring additional Arctic vessel tracking data, among other things, to address this issue. In addition, the Coast Guard's Arctic assets and infrastructure are limited and not suitable for the harsh environment, but the agency is testing equipment and using alternative options to mitigate gaps. Finally, the Coast Guard faces uncertainty over the timing of predicted environmental changes in the Arctic, as well as over future funding streams. To address these challenges the Coast Guard obtains scientific data on Arctic climate change and is studying its Arctic resource requirements to support potential future funding needs.[222]

Coast Guard High Latitude Study Provided to Congress in July 2011

In July 2011, the Coast Guard provided to Congress a study on the Coast Guard's missions and capabilities for operations in high-latitude (i.e., polar) areas. The study, commonly known as the High Latitude Study, is dated July 2010 on its cover. The High Latitude Study concluded the following:

[The study] concludes that future [Coast Guard] capability and capacity gaps will significantly impact four [Coast Guard] mission areas in the Arctic: Defense Readiness, Ice Operations, Marine Environmental Protection, and Ports, Waterways, and Coastal Security. These mission areas address the protection of important national interests in a geographic area where other nations are actively pursuing their own national goals. U.S. national policy and laws define the requirements to assert the nation's jurisdiction over its territory and interests; to ensure the security of its people and critical infrastructure; to participate fully in the collection of scientific knowledge; to support commercial enterprises with public utility; and to ensure that the Arctic environment is not degraded by increased human activity.

The Coast Guard's ability to support Defense Readiness mission requirements in the Arctic is closely linked to DoD responsibilities. The Coast Guard presently possesses the only surface vessels capable of operating in ice-covered and ice-diminished waters. The Coast Guard supports (1) DoD missions such as the resupply of Thule Air Base in Greenland and logistics support (backup) for McMurdo Station in Antarctica and (2) Department of State (DoS) directed Freedom of Navigation Operations. These unique Coast Guard capabilities have been noted by the Joint Chiefs of Staff, the Navy's Task Force Climate Change, and the recently issued Naval Operations Concept 2010.

The common and dominant contributor to these significant mission impacts is the gap in polar icebreaking capability....[223]

---

[222] Government Accountability Office, *Coast Guard[:]Efforts to Identify Arctic Requirements Are Ongoing, but More Communication about Agency Planning Efforts Would Be Beneficial*, GAO-10-870, September 2010, summary page.

[223] For additional discussion, see "Polar Icebreaking".

Other capability gaps contributing to the impact on Coast Guard ability to carry out its missions in the Arctic include:

- Communications System Capability – Continuous coverage along Alaska's West Coast, the Bering Strait, and throughout the North Slope is required for exchanging voice and data communications with Coast Guard units and other government and commercial platforms offshore.

- Forward Operating Locations - No suitable facilities currently exist on the North Slope or near the Bering Strait with facilities sufficient to support extended aircraft servicing and maintenance. Aircraft must travel long distances and expend significant time transiting to and from adequate facilities. This gap reduces on-scene presence and capability to support sustained operations in the region.

- Environmental response in ice-covered waters - The technology and procedures for assessment and mitigation measures for oil spills in ice-covered waters are not fully developed or tested.

Capability gaps in the Arctic region have moderate impacts on [the Coast Guard's] Aids to Navigation (AtoN), Search and Rescue (SAR), and Other Law Enforcement (OLE) missions. Both AtoN and SAR involve the safety of mariners and will gain more importance not only as commerce and tourism cause an increase in maritime traffic, but as U.S. citizens in northern Alaska face more unpredictable conditions. Performance of OLE will be increasingly necessary to ensure the integrity of U.S. living marine resources from outside pressures....

In addition to the assessment of polar icebreaking needs, the Arctic mission analysis examined a set of theoretical mixes (force packages) of Coast Guard assets consisting of icebreakers, their embarked helicopters, and deployment alternatives using aviation forward operating locations in Arctic Alaska....

All [six] of the force mixes [considered in the study] add assets to the existing Coast Guard Alaska Patrol consisting of (1) a high-endurance cutter (not an icebreaker) deployed in the Bering Sea carrying a short range recovery helicopter, and (2) medium range recovery helicopters located at Kodiak in the Gulf of Alaska, and seasonally deployed to locations in Cold Bay and St. Paul Island....

These force packages and associated risk assessment provide a framework for acquisition planning as the Coast Guard implements a strategy for closing the capability gaps. By first recapitalizing the aging icebreakers, the Coast Guard provides a foundation for buildout of these force mixes. In addition to the cost of the icebreakers, the force packages require investment in forward operating locations and in medium range helicopters. The mission analysis reports developed rough order-of-magnitude cost estimates for forward operating locations at approximately $36M [million] each and for helicopters at $9M each....

The analysis shows that the current Coast Guard deployment posture is not capable of effective response in northern Alaska and that response may be improved through a mix of deployed cutters, aircraft, and supporting infrastructure including forward operating locations and communications/navigation systems.[224]

---

[224] *United States Coast Guard High Latitude Region Mission Analysis Capstone Summary*, July 2010, pp. 10-11, 13-15.

U.S.-Canadian Military Cooperation

In December 2009, it was reported that "U.S. and Canadian defense officials are studying emerging gaps in their awareness of Arctic activities, seeking to boost North American Aerospace Defense [NORAD] Command's maritime-warning mission and crafting a new threat assessment for the region." The effort would reportedly involve both NORAD and a Canadian-American advisory board called the Permanent Joint Board on Defense.[225]

In May 2010, it was reported that "American and Canadian defense officials are bolstering collaboration on military exercises, investment plans and technology development related to the Arctic." The report stated that "U.S. and Canadian intelligence officials have created a classified joint "utilization" assessment for the Arctic looking out to 2020, which will be continuously updated." It also stated that "American and Canadian defense officials have just started implementing a new five-year work plan that contains specific initiatives and requires concrete deliverables, Stockton said, noting the Arctic received special attention in the plan. The plan also covers defense critical infrastructure protection, defense support to civil agencies and defense cooperation in the Americas."[226]

January 2009 Arctic Policy Directive

As noted earlier (see "January 2009 Arctic Policy Directive" in "Background" and also "**Error! Reference source not found.**"), the Obama Administration is currently operating under the January 2009 Arctic region policy directive (NSPD 66/HSPD 25) issued by the George W. Bush Administration.[227] Potential oversight questions include but not are limited to the following:

- Is NSPD 66/HSPD 25 a suitable statement of U.S. policy for the Arctic region?[228]

- Although the Obama Administration is currently operating under NSPD 66/HSPD 25, does the Obama Administration fully agree with all parts of it? If not, with which parts does it not fully agree?

- Does the Obama Administration intend to eventually conduct a review of NSDP 66/HSPD 25? If so, what is the Administration's schedule for conducting and releasing the results of that review?

---

[225] Christopher J. Castelli, "DOD, Canada Aim TO Develop Arctic Policy Options By Early 2010," *Inside the Navy*, December 7, 2009.

[226] Christopher J. Castelli, "American, Canadian Defense Officials Tighten Ties On Arctic Issues," *Inside the Navy*, May 3, 2010.

[227] CRS communication with State Department official, October 8, 2010.

[228] On this question, a January 19, 2009, press article about the new directive stated:

> The new policy directive covers several key areas, including national security, energy exploration and the environment, but it does not specify whether any should take precedence over others.

> That led Jeremy Rabkin, a professor at George Mason University Law School, to comment: "It's really a list of all the things we're concerned about; that's not policy. I don't see anything here that helps you decide what gets priority."

> (Juliet Eilperin and Spencer S. Hsu, "White House Directive Guides Policy On Arctic," *Washington Post*, January 19, 2009: 2.)

CRS Reports on Specific Arctic-Related Issues

CRS Report RL34266, *Climate Change: Science Highlights*, by Jane A. Leggett

CRS Report RS21890, *The U.N. Law of the Sea Convention and the United States: Developments Since October 2003*, by Marjorie Ann Browne

CRS Report RL32838, *Arctic National Wildlife Refuge (ANWR): Votes and Legislative Actions Since the 95th Congress*, by M. Lynne Corn and Beth A. Roberts

CRS Report RL34547, *Possible Federal Revenue from Oil Development of ANWR and Nearby Areas*, by Salvatore Lazzari

CRS Report RL33705, *Oil Spills in U.S. Coastal Waters: Background and Governance*, by Jonathan L. Ramseur

CRS Report RL33941, *Polar Bears: Listing Under the Endangered Species Act*, by Eugene H. Buck, M. Lynne Corn, and Kristina Alexander

CRS Report RL34573, *Does the Endangered Species Act Listing Provide More Protection of the Polar Bear?*, by Kristina Alexander

CRS Report RS22906, *Use of the Polar Bear Listing to Force Reduction of Greenhouse Gas Emissions: The Legal Arguments*, by Robert Meltz

CRS Report RL34391, *Coast Guard Polar Icebreaker Modernization: Background and Issues for Congress*, by Ronald O'Rourke

CRS Report RL34342, *Homeland Security: Roles and Missions for United States Northern Command*, by William Knight

Appendix A. Arctic Research and Policy Act (ARPA) of 1984 (Title I of P.L. 98-373)

The text of the Arctic Research and Policy Act (ARPA) of 1984 (Title I of P.L. 98-373 of July 31, 1984[229]) is as follows:

TITLE I – ARCTIC RESEARCH AND POLICY

SHORT TITLE

SEC. 101. This title may be cited as the "Arctic Research and Policy Act of 1984".

FINDINGS AND PURPOSES

SEC. 102. (a) The Congress finds and declares that-

(1) the Arctic, onshore and offshore, contains vital energy resources that can reduce the Nation's dependence on foreign oil and improve the national balance of payments;

(2) as the Nation's only common border with the Soviet Union, the Arctic is critical to national defense;

(3) the renewable resources of the Arctic, specifically fish and other seafood, represent one of the Nation's greatest commercial assets;

(4) Arctic conditions directly affect global weather patterns and must be understood in order to promote better agricultural management throughout the United States;

(5) industrial pollution not originating in the Arctic region collects in the polar air mass, has the potential to disrupt global weather patterns, and must be controlled through international cooperation and consultation;

(6) the Arctic is a natural laboratory for research into human health and adaptation, physical and psychological, to climates of extreme cold and isolation and may provide information crucial for future defense needs;

(7) atmospheric conditions peculiar to the Arctic make the Arctic a unique testing ground for research into high latitude communications, which is likely to be crucial for future defense needs;

(8) Arctic marine technology is critical to cost-effective recovery and transportation of energy resources and to the national defense;

(9) the United States has important security, economic, and environmental interests in developing and maintaining a fleet of icebreaking vessels capable of operating effectively in the heavy ice regions of the Arctic;

---

[229] Title II of P.L. 98-373 is the National Critical Materials Act of 1984.

(10) most Arctic-rim countries, particularly the Soviet Union, possess Arctic technologies far more advanced than those currently available in the United States;

(11) Federal Arctic research is fragmented and uncoordinated at the present time, leading to the neglect of certain areas of research and to unnecessary duplication of effort in other areas of research;

(12) improved logistical coordination and support for Arctic research and better dissemination of research data and information is necessary to increase the efficiency and utility of national Arctic research efforts;

(13) a comprehensive national policy and program plan to organize and fund currently neglected scientific research with respect to the Arctic is necessary to fulfill national objectives in Arctic research;

(14) the Federal Government, in cooperation with State and local governments, should focus its efforts on the collection and characterization of basic data related to biological, materials, geophysical, social, and behavioral phenomena in the Arctic;

(15) research into the long-range health, environmental, and social effects of development in the Arctic is necessary to mitigate the adverse consequences of that development to the land and its residents;

(16) Arctic research expands knowledge of the Arctic, which can enhance the lives of Arctic residents, increase opportunities for international cooperation among Arctic-rim countries, and facilitate the formulation of national policy for the Arctic; and

(17) the Alaskan Arctic provides an essential habitat for marine mammals, migratory waterfowl, and other forms of wildlife which are important to the Nation and which are essential to Arctic residents.

(b) The purposes of this title are-

(1) to establish national policy, priorities, and goals and to provide a Federal program plan for basic and applied scientific research with respect to the Arctic, including natural resources and materials, physical, biological and health sciences, and social and behavioral sciences;

(2) to establish an Arctic Research Commission to promote Arctic research and to recommend Arctic research policy;

(3) to designate the National Science Foundation as the lead agency responsible for implementing Arctic research policy; and

(4) to establish an Interagency Arctic Research Policy Committee to develop a national Arctic research policy and a five year plan to implement that policy.

ARCTIC RESEARCH COMMISSION

SEC. 103. (a) The President shall establish an Arctic Research Commission (hereafter referred to as the "Commission").

(b)(1) The Commission shall be composed of five members appointed by the President, with the Director of the National Science Foundation serving as a nonvoting, ex officio member. The members appointed by the President shall include-

(A) three members appointed from among individuals from academic or other research institutions with expertise in areas of research relating to the Arctic, including the physical, biological, health, environmental, social, and behavioral sciences;

(B) one member appointed from among indigenous residents of the Arctic who are representative of the needs and interests of Arctic residents and who live in areas directly affected by Arctic resource development; and

(C) one member appointed from among individuals familiar with the Arctic and representative of the needs and interests of private industry undertaking resource development in the Arctic.

(2) The President shall designate one of the appointed members of the Commission to be chairperson of the Commission.

(c)(1) Except as provided in paragraph (2) of this subsection, the term of office of each member of the Commission appointed under subsection (b)(1) shall be four years.

(2) Of the members of the Commission originally appointed under subsection (b)(1)-

(A) one shall be appointed for a term of two years;

(B) two shall be appointed for a term of three years; and

(C) two shall be appointed for a term of four years.

(3) Any vacancy occurring in the membership of the Commission shall be filled, after notice of the vacancy is published in the Federal Register, in the manner provided by the preceding provisions of this section, for the remainder of the unexpired term.

(4) A member may serve after the expiration of the member's term of office until the President appoints a successor.

(5) A member may serve consecutive terms beyond the member's original appointment.

(d)(1) Members of the Commission may be allowed travel expenses, including per diem in lieu of subsistence, as authorized by section 5703 of title 5, United States Code. A member of the Commission not presently employed for compensation shall be compensated at a rate equal to the daily equivalent of the rate for GS-16 of the General Schedule under section 5332 of title 5, United States Code, for each day the member is engaged in the actual performance of his duties as a member of the Commission, not to exceed 90 days of service each year. Except for the purposes of chapter 81 of title 5 (relating to compensation for work injuries) and chapter 171 of title 28 (relating to tort claims), a member of the Commission shall not be considered an employee of the United States for any purpose.

(2) The Commission shall meet at the call of its Chairman or a majority of its members.

(3) Each Federal agency referred to in section 107(b) may designate a representative to participate as an observer with the Commission.

These representatives shall report to and advise the Commission on the activities relating to Arctic research of their agencies.

(4) The Commission shall conduct at least one public meeting in the State of Alaska annually.

DUTIES OF COMMISSION

SEC. 104. (a) The Commission shall-

(1) develop and recommend an integrated national Arctic research policy;

(2) in cooperation with the Interagency Arctic Research Policy Committee established under section 107, assist in establishing a national Arctic research program plan to implement the Arctic research policy;

(3) facilitate cooperation between the Federal Government and State and local governments with respect to Arctic research;

(4) review Federal research programs in the Arctic and suggest improvements in coordination among programs;

(5) recommend methods to improve logistical planning and support for Arctic research as may be appropriate and in accordance with the findings and purposes of this title;

(6) suggest methods for improving efficient sharing and dissemination of data and information on the Arctic among interested public and private institutions;

(7) offer other recommendations and advice to the Interagency Committee established under section 107 as it may find appropriate; and

(8) cooperate with the Governor of the State of Alaska and with agencies and organizations of that State which the Governor may designate with respect to the formulation of Arctic research policy.

(b) Not later than January 31 of each year, the Commission shall-

(1) publish a statement of goals and objectives with respect to Arctic research to guide the Interagency Committee established under section 107 in the performance of its duties; and

(2) submit to the President and to the Congress a report describing the activities and accomplishments of the Commission during the immediately preceding fiscal year.

COOPERATION WITH THE COMMISSION

SEC. 105. (a)(1) The Commission may acquire from the head of any Federal agency unclassified data, reports, and other nonproprietary information with respect to Arctic research in the possession of the agency which the Commission considers useful in the discharge of its duties.

(2) Each agency shall cooperate with the Commission and furnish all data, reports, and other information requested by the Commission to the extent permitted by law; except that no agency need furnish any information which it is permitted to withhold under section 552 of title 5, United States Code.

(b) With the consent of the appropriate agency head, the Commission may utilize the facilities and services of any Federal agency to the extent that the facilities and services are needed for the establishment and development of an Arctic research policy, upon reimbursement to be agreed upon by the Commission and the agency head and taking every feasible step to avoid duplication of effort.

(c) All Federal agencies shall consult with the Commission before undertaking major Federal actions relating to Arctic research.

ADMINISTRATION OF THE COMMISSION

SEC. 106. The Commission may-

(1) in accordance with the civil service laws and subchapter III of chapter 53 of title 5, United States Code, appoint and fix the compensation of an Executive Director and necessary additional staff personnel, but not to exceed a total of seven compensated personnel;

(2) procure temporary and intermittent services as authorized by section 3109 of title 5, United States Code;

(3) enter into contracts and procure supplies, services, and personal property; and

(4) enter into agreements with the General Services Administration for the procurement of necessary financial and administrative services, for which payment shall be made by reimbursement from funds of the Commission in amounts to be agreed upon by the Commission and the Administrator of the General Services Administration.

LEAD AGENCY AND INTERAGENCY ARCTIC RESEARCH POLICY COMMITTEE

SEC. 107. (a) The National Science Foundation is designated as the lead agency responsible for implementing Arctic research policy, and the Director of the National Science Foundation shall insure that the requirements of section 108 are fulfilled.

(b)(1) The President shall establish an Interagency Arctic Research Policy Committee (hereinafter referred to as the "Interagency Committee").

(2) The Interagency Committee shall be composed of representatives of the following Federal agencies or offices:

(A) the National Science Foundation;

(B) the Department of Commerce;

(C) the Department of Defense;

(D) the Department of Energy;

(E) the Department of the Interior;

(F) the Department of State;

(G) the Department of Transportation;

(H) the Department of Health and Human Services;

(I) the National Aeronautics and Space Administration;

(J) the Environmental Protection Agency; and

(K) any other agency or office deemed appropriate.

(3) The representative of the National Science Foundation shall serve as the Chairperson of the Interagency Committee.

DUTIES OF THE INTERAGENCY COMMITTEE

SEC. 108. (a) The Interagency Committee shall-

(1) survey Arctic research conducted by Federal, State, and local agencies, universities, and other public and private institutions to help determine priorities for future Arctic research, including natural resources and materials, physical and biological sciences, and social and behavioral sciences;

(2) work with the Commission to develop and establish an integrated national Arctic research policy that will guide Federal agencies in developing and implementing their research programs in the Arctic;

(3) consult with the Commission on-

(A) the development of the national Arctic research policy and the 5-year plan implementing the policy;

(B) Arctic research programs of Federal agencies;

(C) recommendations of the Commission on future Arctic research; and

(D) guidelines for Federal agencies for awarding and administering Arctic research grants;

(4) develop a 5-year plan to implement the national policy, as provided for in section 109;

(5) provide the necessary coordination, data, and assistance for the preparation of a single integrated, coherent, and multiagency budget request for Arctic research as provided for in section 110;

(6) facilitate cooperation between the Federal Government and State and local governments in Arctic research, and recommend the undertaking of neglected areas of research in accordance with the findings and purposes of this title;

(7) coordinate and promote cooperative Arctic scientific research programs with other nations, subject to the foreign policy guidance of the Secretary of State;

(8) cooperate with the Governor of the State of Alaska in fulfilling its responsibilities under this title;

(9) promote Federal interagency coordination of all Arctic research activities, including-

(A) logistical planning and coordination; and

(B) the sharing of data and information associated with Arctic research, subject to section 552 of title 5, United States Code; and

(10) provide public notice of its meetings and an opportunity for the public to participate in the development and implementation of national Arctic research policy.

(b) Not later than January 31, 1986, and biennially thereafter, the Interagency Committee shall submit to the Congress through the President, a brief, concise report containing-

(1) a statement of the activities and accomplishments of the Interagency Committee since its last report; and

(2) a description of the activities of the Commission, detailing with particularity the recommendations of the Commission with respect to Federal activities in Arctic research.

5-YEAR ARCTIC RESEARCH PLAN

SEC. 109. (a) The Interagency Committee, in consultation with the Commission, the Governor of the State of Alaska, the residents of the Arctic, the private sector, and public interest groups, shall prepare a comprehensive 5-year program plan (hereinafter referred to as the "Plan") for the overall Federal effort in Arctic research. The Plan shall be prepared and submitted to the President for transmittal to the Congress within one year after the enactment of this Act and shall be revised biennially thereafter.

(b) The Plan shall contain but need not be limited to the following elements:

(1) an assessment of national needs and problems regarding the Arctic and the research necessary to address those needs or problems;

(2) a statement of the goals and objectives of the Interagency Committee for national Arctic research;

(3) a detailed listing of all existing Federal programs relating to Arctic research, including the existing goals, funding levels for each of the 5 following fiscal years, and the funds currently being expended to conduct the programs;

(4) recommendations for necessary program changes and other proposals to meet the requirements of the policy and goals as set forth by the Commission and in the Plan as currently in effect; and

(5) a description of the actions taken by the Interagency Committee to coordinate the budget review process in order to ensure interagency coordination and cooperation in (A) carrying out Federal Arctic research programs, and (B) eliminating unnecessary duplication of effort among these programs.

COORDINATION AND REVIEW OF BUDGET REQUESTS

SEC. 110. (a) The Office of Science and Technology Policy shall-

(1) review all agency and department budget requests related to the Arctic transmitted pursuant to section 108(a)(5), in accordance with the national Arctic research policy and the 5-year program under section 108(a)(2) and section 109, respectively; and

(2) consult closely with the Interagency Committee and the Commission to guide the Office of Science and Technology Policy's efforts.

(b)(1) The Office of Management and Budget shall consider all Federal agency requests for research related to the Arctic as one integrated, coherent, and multiagency request which shall be reviewed by the Office of Management and Budget prior to submission of the President's annual budget request for its adherence to the Plan. The Commission shall, after submission of the President's annual budget request, review the request and report to Congress on adherence to the Plan.

(2) The Office of Management and Budget shall seek to facilitate planning for the design, procurement, maintenance, deployment, and operations of icebreakers needed to provide a platform for Arctic research by allocating all funds necessary to support icebreaking operations, except for recurring incremental costs associated with specific projects, to the Coast Guard.

AUTHORIZATION OF APPROPRIATIONS; NEW SPENDING AUTHORITY

SEC. 111. (a) There are authorized to be appropriated such sums as may be necessary for carrying out this title.

(b) Any new spending authority (within the meaning of section 401 of the Congressional Budget Act of 1974) which is provided under this title shall be effective for any fiscal year only to such extent or in such amounts as may be provided in appropriation Acts.

DEFINITION

SEC. 112. As used in this title, the term "Arctic" means all United States and foreign territory north of the Arctic Circle and all United States territory north and west of the boundary formed by the Porcupine, Yukon, and Kuskokwim Rivers; all contiguous seas, including the Arctic Ocean and the Beaufort, Bering, and Chukchi Seas; and the Aleutian chain.

Appendix B. P.L. 101-609 of 1990, Amending Arctic Research and Policy Act (ARPA) of 1984

The Arctic Research and Policy Act (ARPA) of 1984 (see **Appendix A**) was amended by P.L. 101-609 of November 16, 1990. The text of P.L. 101-609 is as follows:

SECTION 1. Except as specifically provided in this Act, whenever in this Act an amendment or repeal is expressed as an amendment to, or repeal of a provision, the reference shall be deemed to be made to the Arctic Research and Policy Act of 1984.

SEC. 2. Section 103(b)(1) (15 U.S.C. 4102(b)(1)) is amended—

(1) in the text above clause (A), by striking out `five' and inserting in lieu thereof `seven';

(2) in clause (A), by striking out `three' and inserting in lieu thereof `four'; and

(3) in clause (C), by striking out `one member' and inserting in lieu thereof `two members'.

SEC. 3. Section 103(d)(1) (15 U.S.C. 4102(d)(1)) is amended by striking out `GS-16' and inserting in lieu thereof `GS-18'.

SEC. 4. (a) Section 104(a) (15 U.S.C. 4102(a)) is amended—

(1) in paragraph (4), by striking out `suggest' and inserting in lieu thereof `recommend';

(2) in paragraph (6), by striking out `suggest' and inserting in lieu thereof `recommend';

(3) in paragraph (7), by striking out `and' at the end thereof;

(4) in paragraph (8), by striking out the period and inserting in lieu thereof a semicolon; and

(5) by adding at the end thereof the following new paragraphs:

`(9) recommend to the Interagency Committee the means for developing international scientific cooperation in the Arctic; and

`(10) not later than January 31, 1991, and every 2 years thereafter, publish a statement of goals and objectives with respect to Arctic research to guide the Interagency Committee established under section 107 in the performance of its duties.'.

(b) Section 104(b) is amended to read as follows:

`(b) Not later than January 31 of each year, the Commission shall submit to the President and to the Congress a report describing the activities and accomplishments of the Commission during the immediately preceding fiscal year.'.

SEC. 5. Section 106 (15 U.S.C. 4105) is amended—

(1) in paragraph (3), by striking out `and' at the end thereof;

(2) in paragraph (4), by striking out the period at the end thereof and inserting in lieu thereof '; and'; and

(3) by adding at the end thereof the following new paragraph:

'(5) appoint, and accept without compensation the services of, scientists and engineering specialists to be advisors to the Commission. Each advisor may be allowed travel expenses, including per diem in lieu of subsistence, as authorized by section 5703 of title 5, United States Code. Except for the purposes of chapter 81 of title 5 (relating to compensation for work injuries) and chapter 171 of title 28 (relating to tort claims) of the United States Code, an advisor appointed under this paragraph shall not be considered an employee of the United States for any purpose.'.

SEC. 6. Subsection (b)(2) of section 108 (15 U.S.C. 4107(b)(2)) is amended to read as follows:

'(2) a statement detailing with particularity the recommendations of the Commission with respect to Federal interagency activities in Arctic research and the disposition and responses to those recommendations.'.

Appendix C. January 2009 Arctic Policy Directive (NSPD 66/HSPD 25)

On January 12, 2009, the George W. Bush Administration released a presidential directive establishing a new U.S. policy for the Arctic region. The directive, dated January 9, 2009, was issued as National Security Presidential Directive 66/Homeland Security Presidential Directive 25 (NSPD 66/HSPD 25). The text of NSPD 66/HSPD 25 is as follows:

SUBJECT: Arctic Region Policy

I. PURPOSE

A. This directive establishes the policy of the United States with respect to the Arctic region and directs related implementation actions. This directive supersedes Presidential Decision Directive/NSC-26 (PDD-26; issued 1994) with respect to Arctic policy but not Antarctic policy; PDD-26 remains in effect for Antarctic policy only.

B. This directive shall be implemented in a manner consistent with the Constitution and laws of the United States, with the obligations of the United States under the treaties and other international agreements to which the United States is a party, and with customary international law as recognized by the United States, including with respect to the law of the sea.

II. BACKGROUND

A. The United States is an Arctic nation, with varied and compelling interests in that region. This directive takes into account several developments, including, among others:

1. Altered national policies on homeland security and defense;

2. The effects of climate change and increasing human activity in the Arctic region;

3. The establishment and ongoing work of the Arctic Council; and

4. A growing awareness that the Arctic region is both fragile and rich in resources.

III. POLICY

A. It is the policy of the United States to:

1. Meet national security and homeland security needs relevant to the Arctic region;

2. Protect the Arctic environment and conserve its biological resources;

3. Ensure that natural resource management and economic development in the region are environmentally sustainable;

4. Strengthen institutions for cooperation among the eight Arctic nations (the United States, Canada, Denmark, Finland, Iceland, Norway, the Russian Federation, and Sweden);

5. Involve the Arctic's indigenous communities in decisions that affect them; and

6. Enhance scientific monitoring and research into local, regional, and global environmental issues.

B. National Security and Homeland Security Interests in the Arctic

1. The United States has broad and fundamental national security interests in the Arctic region and is prepared to operate either independently or in conjunction with other states to safeguard these interests. These interests include such matters as missile defense and early warning; deployment of sea and air systems for strategic sealift, strategic deterrence, maritime presence, and maritime security operations; and ensuring freedom of navigation and overflight.

2. The United States also has fundamental homeland security interests in preventing terrorist attacks and mitigating those criminal or hostile acts that could increase the United States vulnerability to terrorism in the Arctic region.

3. The Arctic region is primarily a maritime domain; as such, existing policies and authorities relating to maritime areas continue to apply, including those relating to law enforcement.[1] Human activity in the Arctic region is increasing and is projected to increase further in coming years. This requires the United States to assert a more active and influential national presence to protect its Arctic interests and to project sea power throughout the region.

4. The United States exercises authority in accordance with lawful claims of United States sovereignty, sovereign rights, and jurisdiction in the Arctic region, including sovereignty within the territorial sea, sovereign rights and jurisdiction within the United States exclusive economic zone and on the continental shelf, and appropriate control in the United States contiguous zone.

5. Freedom of the seas is a top national priority. The Northwest Passage is a strait used for international navigation, and the Northern Sea Route includes straits used for international navigation; the regime of transit passage applies to passage through those straits. Preserving the rights and duties relating to navigation and overflight in the Arctic region supports our ability to exercise these rights throughout the world, including through strategic straits.

6. Implementation: In carrying out this policy as it relates to national security and homeland security interests in the Arctic, the Secretaries of State, Defense, and Homeland Security, in coordination with heads of other relevant executive departments and agencies, shall:

a. Develop greater capabilities and capacity, as necessary, to protect United States air, land, and sea borders in the Arctic region;

b. Increase Arctic maritime domain awareness in order to protect maritime commerce, critical infrastructure, and key resources;

c. Preserve the global mobility of United States military and civilian vessels and aircraft throughout the Arctic region;

d. Project a sovereign United States maritime presence in the Arctic in support of essential United States interests; and

e. Encourage the peaceful resolution of disputes in the Arctic region.

C. International Governance

1. The United States participates in a variety of fora, international organizations, and bilateral contacts that promote United States interests in the Arctic. These include the Arctic Council, the International Maritime Organization (IMO), wildlife conservation and management agreements, and many other mechanisms. As the Arctic changes and human activity in the region increases, the United States and other governments should consider, as appropriate, new international arrangements or enhancements to existing arrangements.

2. The Arctic Council has produced positive results for the United States by working within its limited mandate of environmental protection and sustainable development. Its subsidiary bodies, with help from many United States agencies, have developed and undertaken projects on a wide range of topics. The Council also provides a beneficial venue for interaction with indigenous groups. It is the position of the United States that the Arctic Council should remain a high-level forum devoted to issues within its current mandate and not be transformed into a formal international organization, particularly one with assessed contributions. The United States is nevertheless open to updating the structure of the Council, including consolidation of, or making operational changes to, its subsidiary bodies, to the extent such changes can clearly improve the Council's work and are consistent with the general mandate of the Council.

3. The geopolitical circumstances of the Arctic region differ sufficiently from those of the Antarctic region such that an "Arctic Treaty" of broad scope—along the lines of the Antarctic Treaty—is not appropriate or necessary.

4. The Senate should act favorably on U.S. accession to the U.N. Convention on the Law of the Sea promptly, to protect and advance U.S. interests, including with respect to the Arctic. Joining will serve the national security interests of the United States, including the maritime mobility of our Armed Forces worldwide. It will secure U.S. sovereign rights over extensive marine areas, including the valuable natural resources they contain. Accession will promote U.S. interests in the environmental health of the oceans. And it will give the United States a seat at the table when the rights that are vital to our interests are debated and interpreted.

5. Implementation: In carrying out this policy as it relates to international governance, the Secretary of State, in coordination with heads of other relevant executive departments and agencies, shall:

a. Continue to cooperate with other countries on Arctic issues through the United Nations (U.N.) and its specialized agencies, as well as through treaties such as the U.N. Framework Convention on Climate Change, the Convention on International Trade in Endangered Species of Wild Fauna and Flora, the Convention on Long Range Transboundary Air Pollution and its protocols, and the Montreal Protocol on Substances that Deplete the Ozone Layer;

b. Consider, as appropriate, new or enhanced international arrangements for the Arctic to address issues likely to arise from expected increases in human activity in that region, including shipping, local development and subsistence, exploitation of living marine resources, development of energy and other resources, and tourism;

c. Review Arctic Council policy recommendations developed within the ambit of the Council's scientific reviews and ensure the policy recommendations are subject to review by Arctic governments; and

d. Continue to seek advice and consent of the United States Senate to accede to the 1982 Law of the Sea Convention.

D. Extended Continental Shelf and Boundary Issues

1.   Defining with certainty the area of the Arctic seabed and subsoil in which the United States may exercise its sovereign rights over natural resources such as oil, natural gas, methane hydrates, minerals, and living marine species is critical to our national interests in energy security, resource management, and environmental protection. The most effective way to achieve international recognition and legal certainty for our extended continental shelf is through the procedure available to States Parties to the U.N. Convention on the Law of the Sea.

2.   The United States and Canada have an unresolved boundary in the Beaufort Sea. United States policy recognizes a boundary in this area based on equidistance. The United States recognizes that the boundary area may contain oil, natural gas, and other resources.

3.   The United States and Russia are abiding by the terms of a maritime boundary treaty concluded in 1990, pending its entry into force. The United States is prepared to enter the agreement into force once ratified by the Russian Federation.

4.   Implementation: In carrying out this policy as it relates to extended continental shelf and boundary issues, the Secretary of State, in coordination with heads of other relevant executive departments and agencies, shall:

a.   Take all actions necessary to establish the outer limit of the continental shelf appertaining to the United States, in the Arctic and in other regions, to the fullest extent permitted under international law;

b.   Consider the conservation and management of natural resources during the process of delimiting the extended continental shelf; and

c.   Continue to urge the Russian Federation to ratify the 1990 United States-Russia maritime boundary agreement.

E. Promoting International Scientific Cooperation

1.   Scientific research is vital for the promotion of United States interests in the Arctic region. Successful conduct of U.S. research in the Arctic region requires access throughout the Arctic Ocean and to terrestrial sites, as well as viable international mechanisms for sharing access to research platforms and timely exchange of samples, data, and analyses. Better coordination with the Russian Federation, facilitating access to its domain, is particularly important.

2.   The United States promotes the sharing of Arctic research platforms with other countries in support of collaborative research that advances fundamental understanding of the Arctic region in general and potential Arctic change in particular. This could include collaboration with bodies such as the Nordic Council and the European Polar Consortium, as well as with individual nations.

3.   Accurate prediction of future environmental and climate change on a regional basis, and the delivery of near real-time information to end-users, requires obtaining, analyzing, and disseminating accurate data from the entire Arctic region, including both paleoclimatic data and observational data. The United States has made significant investments in the infrastructure needed to collect environmental data in the Arctic region, including the establishment of portions of an Arctic circumpolar observing network through a partnership among United States agencies, academic collaborators, and Arctic residents. The United States promotes active involvement of all Arctic nations in these efforts in order to advance

scientific understanding that could provide the basis for assessing future impacts and proposed response strategies.

4.   United States platforms capable of supporting forefront research in the Arctic Ocean, including portions expected to be ice-covered for the foreseeable future, as well as seasonally ice-free regions, should work with those of other nations through the establishment of an Arctic circumpolar observing network. All Arctic nations are members of the Group on Earth Observations partnership, which provides a framework for organizing an international approach to environmental observations in the region. In addition, the United States recognizes that academic and research institutions are vital partners in promoting and conducting Arctic research.

5.   Implementation: In carrying out this policy as it relates to promoting scientific international cooperation, the Secretaries of State, the Interior, and Commerce and the Director of the National Science Foundation, in coordination with heads of other relevant executive departments and agencies, shall:

a.   Continue to play a leadership role in research throughout the Arctic region;

b.   Actively promote full and appropriate access by scientists to Arctic research sites through bilateral and multilateral measures and by other means;

c.   Lead the effort to establish an effective Arctic circumpolar observing network with broad partnership from other relevant nations;

d.   Promote regular meetings of Arctic science ministers or research council heads to share information concerning scientific research opportunities and to improve coordination of international Arctic research programs;

e.   Work with the Interagency Arctic Research Policy Committee (IARPC) to promote research that is strategically linked to U.S. policies articulated in this directive, with input from the Arctic Research Commission; and

f.   Strengthen partnerships with academic and research institutions and build upon the relationships these institutions have with their counterparts in other nations.

F. Maritime Transportation in the Arctic Region

1.   The United States priorities for maritime transportation in the Arctic region are:

a.   To facilitate safe, secure, and reliable navigation;

b.   To protect maritime commerce; and

c.   To protect the environment.

2.   Safe, secure, and environmentally sound maritime commerce in the Arctic region depends on infrastructure to support shipping activity, search and rescue capabilities, short- and long-range aids to navigation, high-risk area vessel-traffic management, iceberg warnings and other sea ice information, effective shipping standards, and measures to protect the marine environment. In addition, effective search and rescue in the Arctic will require local, State, Federal, tribal, commercial, volunteer, scientific, and multinational cooperation.

3.   Working through the International Maritime Organization (IMO), the United States promotes strengthening existing measures and, as necessary, developing new measures to improve the safety and security of maritime transportation, as well as to protect the marine environment in the Arctic region. These measures may include ship routing and reporting systems, such as traffic separation and vessel traffic management schemes in Arctic chokepoints; updating and strengthening of the Guidelines for Ships Operating in Arctic Ice-Covered Waters; underwater noise standards for commercial shipping; a review of shipping insurance issues; oil and other hazardous material pollution response agreements; and environmental standards.

4.   Implementation: In carrying out this policy as it relates to maritime transportation in the Arctic region, the Secretaries of State, Defense, Transportation, Commerce, and Homeland Security, in coordination with heads of other relevant executive departments and agencies, shall:

a.   Develop additional measures, in cooperation with other nations, to address issues that are likely to arise from expected increases in shipping into, out of, and through the Arctic region;

b.   Commensurate with the level of human activity in the region, establish a risk-based capability to address hazards in the Arctic environment. Such efforts shall advance work on pollution prevention and response standards; determine basing and logistics support requirements, including necessary airlift and icebreaking capabilities; and improve plans and cooperative agreements for search and rescue;

c.   Develop Arctic waterways management regimes in accordance with accepted international standards, including vessel traffic-monitoring and routing; safe navigation standards; accurate and standardized charts; and accurate and timely environmental and navigational information; and

d.   Evaluate the feasibility of using access through the Arctic for strategic sealift and humanitarian aid and disaster relief.

G. Economic Issues, Including Energy

1.   Sustainable development in the Arctic region poses particular challenges. Stakeholder input will inform key decisions as the United States seeks to promote economic and energy security. Climate change and other factors are significantly affecting the lives of Arctic inhabitants, particularly indigenous communities. The United States affirms the importance to Arctic communities of adapting to climate change, given their particular vulnerabilities.

2.   Energy development in the Arctic region will play an important role in meeting growing global energy demand as the area is thought to contain a substantial portion of the world's undiscovered energy resources. The United States seeks to ensure that energy development throughout the Arctic occurs in an environmentally sound manner, taking into account the interests of indigenous and local communities, as well as open and transparent market principles. The United States seeks to balance access to, and development of, energy and other natural resources with the protection of the Arctic environment by ensuring that continental shelf resources are managed in a responsible manner and by continuing to work closely with other Arctic nations.

3.   The United States recognizes the value and effectiveness of existing fora, such as the Arctic Council, the International Regulators Forum, and the International Standards Organization.

4.   Implementation: In carrying out this policy as it relates to economic issues, including energy, the Secretaries of State, the Interior, Commerce, and Energy, in coordination with heads of other relevant executive departments and agencies, shall:

a.   Seek to increase efforts, including those in the Arctic Council, to study changing climate conditions, with a view to preserving and enhancing economic opportunity in the Arctic region. Such efforts shall include inventories and assessments of villages, indigenous communities, subsistence opportunities, public facilities, infrastructure, oil and gas development projects, alternative energy development opportunities, forestry, cultural and other sites, living marine resources, and other elements of the Arctic's socioeconomic composition;

b.   Work with other Arctic nations to ensure that hydrocarbon and other development in the Arctic region is carried out in accordance with accepted best practices and internationally recognized standards and the 2006 Group of Eight (G-8) Global Energy Security Principles;

c.   Consult with other Arctic nations to discuss issues related to exploration, production, environmental and socioeconomic impacts, including drilling conduct, facility sharing, the sharing of environmental data, impact assessments, compatible monitoring programs, and reservoir management in areas with potentially shared resources;

d.   Protect United States interests with respect to hydrocarbon reservoirs that may overlap boundaries to mitigate adverse environmental and economic consequences related to their development;

e.   Identify opportunities for international cooperation on methane hydrate issues, North Slope hydrology, and other matters;

f.   Explore whether there is a need for additional fora for informing decisions on hydrocarbon leasing, exploration, development, production, and transportation, as well as shared support activities, including infrastructure projects; and

g.   Continue to emphasize cooperative mechanisms with nations operating in the region to address shared concerns, recognizing that most known Arctic oil and gas resources are located outside of United States jurisdiction.

H. Environmental Protection and Conservation of Natural Resources

1.   The Arctic environment is unique and changing. Increased human activity is expected to bring additional stressors to the Arctic environment, with potentially serious consequences for Arctic communities and ecosystems.

2.   Despite a growing body of research, the Arctic environment remains poorly understood. Sea ice and glaciers are in retreat. Permafrost is thawing and coasts are eroding. Pollutants from within and outside the Arctic are contaminating the region. Basic data are lacking in many fields. High levels of uncertainty remain concerning the effects of climate change and increased human activity in the Arctic. Given the need for decisions to be based on sound scientific and socioeconomic information, Arctic environmental research, monitoring, and vulnerability assessments are top priorities. For example, an understanding of the probable consequences of global climate variability and change on Arctic ecosystems is essential to guide the effective long-term management of Arctic natural resources and to address socioeconomic impacts of changing patterns in the use of natural resources.

3.   Taking into account the limitations in existing data, United States efforts to protect the Arctic environment and to conserve its natural resources must be risk-based and proceed on the basis of the best available information.

4.   The United States supports the application in the Arctic region of the general principles of international fisheries management outlined in the 1995 Agreement for the Implementation of the Provisions of the United Nations Convention on the Law of the Sea of December 10, 1982, relating to the Conservation and Management of Straddling Fish Stocks and Highly Migratory Fish Stocks and similar instruments. The United States endorses the protection of vulnerable marine ecosystems in the Arctic from destructive fishing practices and seeks to ensure an adequate enforcement presence to safeguard Arctic living marine resources.

5.   With temperature increases in the Arctic region, contaminants currently locked in the ice and soils will be released into the air, water, and land. This trend, along with increased human activity within and below the Arctic, will result in increased introduction of contaminants into the Arctic, including both persistent pollutants (e.g., persistent organic pollutants and mercury) and airborne pollutants (e.g., soot).

6.   Implementation: In carrying out this policy as it relates to environmental protection and conservation of natural resources, the Secretaries of State, the Interior, Commerce, and Homeland Security and the Administrator of the Environmental Protection Agency, in coordination with heads of other relevant executive departments and agencies, shall:

a.   In cooperation with other nations, respond effectively to increased pollutants and other environmental challenges;

b.   Continue to identify ways to conserve, protect, and sustainably manage Arctic species and ensure adequate enforcement presence to safeguard living marine resources, taking account of the changing ranges or distribution of some species in the Arctic. For species whose range includes areas both within and beyond United States jurisdiction, the United States shall continue to collaborate with other governments to ensure effective conservation and management;

c.   Seek to develop ways to address changing and expanding commercial fisheries in the Arctic, including through consideration of international agreements or organizations to govern future Arctic fisheries;

d.   Pursue marine ecosystem-based management in the Arctic; and

e.   Intensify efforts to develop scientific information on the adverse effects of pollutants on human health and the environment and work with other nations to reduce the introduction of key pollutants into the Arctic.

IV. Resources and Assets

A.   Implementing a number of the policy elements directed above will require appropriate resources and assets. These elements shall be implemented consistent with applicable law and authorities of agencies, or heads of agencies, vested by law, and subject to the availability of appropriations. The heads of executive departments and agencies with responsibilities relating to the Arctic region shall work to identify future budget, administrative, personnel, or legislative proposal requirements to implement the elements of this directive.

[1] These policies and authorities include Freedom of Navigation (PDD/NSC-32), the U.S. Policy on Protecting the Ocean Environment (PDD/NSC-36), Maritime Security Policy (NSPD-41/HSPD-13), and the National Strategy for Maritime Security (NSMS).[230]

Author Contact Information

Ronald O'Rourke, Coordinator
Specialist in Naval Affairs
rorourke@crs.loc.gov, 7-7610

Marjorie Ann Browne
Specialist in International Relations
mbrowne@crs.loc.gov, 7-7695

Eugene H. Buck
Specialist in Natural Resources Policy
gbuck@crs.loc.gov, 7-7262

M. Lynne Corn
Specialist in Natural Resources Policy
lcorn@crs.loc.gov, 7-7267

Carl Ek
Specialist in International Relations
cek@crs.loc.gov, 7-7286

Peter Folger
Specialist in Energy and Natural Resources Policy
pfolger@crs.loc.gov, 7-1517

John Frittelli
Specialist in Transportation Policy
jfrittelli@crs.loc.gov, 7-7033

Curry L. Hagerty
Specialist in Energy and Natural Resources Policy
chagerty@crs.loc.gov, 7-7738

Marc Humphries
Specialist in Energy Policy
mhumphries@crs.loc.gov, 7-7264

Jane A. Leggett
Specialist in Energy and Environmental Policy
jaleggett@crs.loc.gov, 7-9525

Jonathan L. Ramseur
Specialist in Environmental Policy
jramseur@crs.loc.gov, 7-7919

---

[230] Source for text: http://fas.org/irp/offdocs/nspd/nspd-66.htm. The text is also available online at http://www.nsf.gov/od/opp/opp_advisory/briefings/may2009/nspd66_hspd25.pdf.

www.ingramcontent.com/pod-product-compliance
Lightning Source LLC
Chambersburg PA
CBHW070553290526
45790CB00002B/669